PERIODIZ
FITNESS TRAINING

A REVOLUTIONARY FOOTBALL CONDITIONING PROGRAM

WRITTEN BY
JAVIER MALLO

PUBLISHED BY

PERIODIZATION FITNESS TRAINING

A REVOLUTIONARY FOOTBALL CONDITIONING PROGRAM

First Published July 2014 by SoccerTutor.com
Info@soccertutor.com | www.SoccerTutor.com

UK: 0208 1234 007 | **US:** (305) 767 4443 | **ROTW:** +44 208 1234 007

ISBN: 978-0-9576705-6-3

Author

Javier Mallo

Original Spanish Publishers

This book is an adapted version based on the book "La preparación (física) para el fútbol basada en el Juego", which was published in Spanish by the editor Futboldelibro in February 2013.

Edited by

Alex Fitzgerald - SoccerTutor.com

Cover Design by

Alex Macrides, Think Out Of The Box Ltd.
Email: design@thinkootb.com Tel: +44 (0) 208 144 3550

Diagrams

Diagram designs by SoccerTutor.com. All the diagrams in this book have been created using SoccerTutor.com Tactics Manager Software available from www.SoccerTutor.com

Note: While every effort has been made to ensure the technical accuracy of the content of this book, neither the author nor publishers can accept any responsibility for any injury or loss sustained as a result of the use of this material.

CONTENTS

MEET THE AUTHOR
REAL MADRID FITNESS COACH

JAVIER MALLO
Real Madrid Fitness Coach

Previous Coaching positions:

- Sports Scientist/Strength & Conditioning Coach at Manchester City 2011-2013 (2 seasons)
- Fitness Coach at Atletico de Madrid for 4 seasons
- Fitness Coach and Assistant Coach at U.D. San Sebastian de los Reyes (Spain, Division 2B) for 6 seasons

Credentials:

- UEFA A Coaching Licence
- PhD in Sports Sciences
  (Sport Sciences Faculty -INEF- Technical University of Madrid)
- MSc in High Performance in Sports
- BSc in Physiotherapy

Additional Information:

- Associate Professor lecturing Football at the Sports Sciences Faculty of the Technical University of Madrid for 3 years
- Doctorate (PhD) research studentship/scholarship at the Sports Sciences Faculty of the Technical University of Madrid for 4 years
- More than 20 papers published in international peer-review journals, such as the Journal of Sports Sciences, International Journal of Sports Medicine, Journal of Sports Sciences and Medicine, Journal of Strength, Conditioning Research, and many more
- Key-note speaker in various different international congresses and courses about Football

WHAT IS PERIODIZATION AND HOW CAN THIS BOOK HELP ME?

What is Periodization?

Periodization is the systematic planning of fitness training. It is understood as the organisation of the season into smaller periods and units (Issurin, 2008) to optimise training.

Planning our fitness training this way helps us to make sure that the correct intensity and duration of our practices is used at the different stages of a season i.e. pre-season and different periods of the competitive schedule.

How Can Periodization Benefit a Team?

Periodization helps a coach to select the best moments to introduce certain types of training practices. That is, once the coach has all the correct pieces (training practices with details of complexity, duration and intensity), periodization would help them to build the puzzle.

Within this book we provide fitness training which includes practices that develop all the attributes needed for an individual and a team:

- Warm Ups with and without the Ball
- Conditioning
- Technical
- Tactical
- Competitive Small Sided Games
- Attacking
- Defending
- The Transition Phases; from Defence to Attack and Attack to Defence

Why Use It for Fitness Training?

Training periodization tries to solve the problem of organising the training loads in order to achieve the highest team performance possible at the different stages of a season. The season can also be divided into smaller temporal units such as phases, cycles, blocks, etc.

When thinking about a training week (short term plans), the loads can be periodized for the interval of time between two competitive matches. These micro-cycles are explained fully in chapter 3.

FOREWARD
by Chema Sanz, professional Fitness Coach

During the last decades many things have changed in sport and, particularly, in football. New theories have arisen during the 20th century which provoked a substantial modification in the way we understand training in collective sports. Football, as a collective sport, and the footballer, as a living being, form part of what the new theories define as complex systems. A complex system is a group of elements which interact between them to achieve a common objective. From this affirmation it can be inferred that a change in any of the elements would inexorably affect the remaining. To understand their behaviour we need to know not only their components, but also the relationships between them. We should never analyse them in isolated parts but as an interdependent phenomenon. The properties and training of a football team belong to a whole, and none of the parts can be treated by themselves. The players will always present different performances depending on the context they are in.

In the course of this book the author will help us (practically) to bring light to football´s knowledge, providing us with a different perspective to observe the events which form part of the training process. During these pages he will show us that coaches require a systemic and integral perspective of all the elements that might influence performance, to confront all the difficulties that preparing and optimising the capacities and potentialities of a football team presents. Training organisation must follow a holistic approach (the observation of an event from a functional point of view considering all the parts and their interrelationship between them) and, for instance, a more correct view of the phenomenon we want to observe and know about.

This is the line adopted by the author who, observing the team properties from its totality and respecting the interaction of components, delves into what happens during the training process of a football team, putting a great effort to study its systemic character.

This new vision has allowed a qualitative leap forward in football´s training methodology, setting the team's tactical organisation as the primary aim. Training is growing from the game, for the game and from the necessities that players have to play the game.

This detailed study will allow us to develop our capacities to design the optimum training practices to best suit the competitive reality of our team. It is a really easy-to-read book, enjoyable and will help you to better understand the organisation of the different elements that form part of the training process, using reflection as a permanent tool. Javi Mallo is a football man who has the advantage of having experienced the game from different angles. As all lively and fervent people do, he has been constantly evolving, growing and maturing during his career as a coach.

This book is an invitation to keep moving forward, to revise all the acquired knowledge and jump on board to develop new knowledge. As a summary, this boom can help us to keep growing and to increase our qualitative value as coaches. In addition, reading the book will enrich us with interesting suggestions which would ease decision making and problem solving situations in our teams. If there is something I would like to highlight from this detailed and thorough book, it is the total practical application, joining theoretical rigour and practical implications and, even more importantly, it uses a football specific context to circumscribe fitness training.

Finally, I would like to express my sincere acknowledgement to the author for having dedicated his thinking and effort to give us the opportunity of knowing more, close to the field, about this marvellous game known as football.

The formation process is restless, open 24 hours per day and 365 days a year.

Chema Sanz

Former fitness coach at the following clubs:

- Mallorca
- Deportivo de la Coruña
- Almería
- Tenerife
- Real Madrid Castilla
- Terrasa
- Ciudad de Murcia
- Oviedo
- Levante.

FOREWARD

by Javier Sampedro Molinuevo, Dean of the Sport Sciences Faculty

"Tactics consists in knowing what to do when there is something to do and strategy is knowing what to do when there is nothing to do". In other words, "tactics is a short-term movement which allows taking one position and strategy is the way to win the game".
"El ocho" S. Tarta Kowe (1887-1956). Great Polish chess master.

I have been asked to write a short preface to the book you have in your hands, which represents a great pleasure for myself at the same time as a responsibility. I have known the author from his beginning as a student in the Sport Sciences Faculty (INEF) of the Technical University of Madrid, where he already showed curiosity and reflection about everything that interested him, which was mainly related to football.

Some years later, Javier took part in the postgraduate courses with his inseparable classmate Abraham Garcia (son of the successful football coach Juanjo Garcia, who took Real Madrid Castilla to the final of the Spanish Cup and to European competition). It was an honour for me to be the Chairman of his PhD dissertation which, by the way, was brilliantly done. During the following years he was an associate professor in the Faculty, but I already knew that what Javier wanted was to be close to the field of play, involved in the day-to-day training and competition. His constant curiosity for learning and academic bravery has led him to write this book, trying to show how the perspective to understand the game has changed in the actual days.

Leaving to one side the biographic and more personal data, we can go deep into the details of the present book. To create or do science is not easy, but the author respects three necessary conditions to be able to do so. The important factors are having a clear object of study, having a knowledge area for where to apply it and using an appropriate scientific methodology. The author respects the nature of notational game analysis and adopts a bottom up

perspective, that is, based on observing the reality of the playing action; from practice to theory and not the other way around.

Football must be interpreted from an ecological perspective, like a system, with many interactions between the internal and external game elements. Everything needs to be ordered respecting the Chaos and the Complex Systems Theory. The game definition must be dynamic and changeable, where any modification in a situation, as minor as it might seem, modifies the following and creates a new situation with its own properties and identity. I agree with this consideration and interpretation of modern football, where a mathematical approach to playing patterns can help us to understand it. The validity of a text and its scientific weight, as the one we are talking about, is given by the abundant references which the author uses, which we think are pertinent and adequate.

We cannot forget to mention the author's CV, with numerous peer-reviewed published papers in the international scientific literature which support his previous knowledge. At the same time, this background is balanced with his professional experience in different clubs, even internationally at Manchester City, during the last seasons.

After carefully reading the book I believe the Introduction perfectly justifies the problem and creates a clear and well measured position about the actual conception of game analysis. This allows creating clear ideas which go beyond classical phrases such as "football is football", "everything has already

Periodization Fitness Training

been invented", "it is impossible to apply theory to football", "football is different" and so on. We still have to respect that chance can generate a disturbing effect in football, but we should not use this to stop rationalising each situation. We agree with the idea that reflecting on the doubts that come from game analysis and the constant search for certainties should move us to take hand by hand theory and practice, sharing a common and understandable language independently of the previous knowledge.

The author uses an opportune logical argument to provide a solution to his daily work on the field. This book is original and its graphics and illustrations are based on his daily training activities and realistic observations of match play, which are Javier's best weapons. The fitness coach is introducing more practices based on game analysis nowadays, searching to simultaneously develop the physical and tactical (decision making) capacities.

Javier respects the game´s internal logic by creating a methodological order when describing the training practices, which always respect the specifics of the game. The book content is reduced to four chapters, including an excellent third chapter with plenty of recent and valid references. We have to acknowledge the editor for publishing this book and for giving, in these complicated times, the opportunity for young talents to express themselves. We mainly agree with all the contents of the book and the small discordances will remain for debate between the author and myself.

As happens to all of us researchers, doubt will always remain present and what today looks like a solid and firm paradigm, tomorrow might be not as clear, so we need to evolve and adapt to the new situations. Only by having an open mind can we understand the pathways of the application of science in football. I know that in this sport, over all the other ones, being considered as a scientist sometimes seems inappropriate, but I am the kind of person who believes in the necessity of having an open-minded approach to football training.

In all the teams the author Javier Mallo has worked at during all these years he has left the stamp of his knowledge and, even more importantly, efficiency when applying general and specific solutions for practical situations, as difficult as they can be.

I wish you, Javier, all the best, that will always take you to success.

Javier Sampedro Molinuevo

- Dean of the Sport Sciences Faculty
- Professor of the Technical University of Madrid

INTRODUCTION

Does Fitness Training in Football Exist?

This sudden question interrupts the hum of voices in the auditorium. For a short time, silence dominates the room. In some places, the sole formulation of this question turned out to be a sacrilege and the answers rushed. In other environments, the responses were not as conclusive which allowed new pathways to be established for the debate. In almost parallel circumstances, hundreds of miles away, similar comments about these aspects were made out loud (Pol, 2011). It is impossible to advance your knowledge without analysing doubt about previous experiences.

Will Fitness Training in Football Exist in 10 Years Time?

The silence is now longer and impenetrable. Affirmations cannot be as categorical as they were before. Football is a permanently dynamic body and it is highly risky to set certainties regarding its evolution. It is possible that in the future a part of training may be known as fitness or conditioning, but what different professionals might understand from it will be very different. Football will always remain the same sport, but the way it is played will present many varied alternatives and directions in respect to the approach to training.

Research and Studies

This book tries to organise and analyse thoughts from the different sides of football in the last decade. The more theoretical knowledge was acquired studying Physical Activity and Sport Sciences (INEF) at the Technical University of Madrid (first as a student of the Degree, later holding a PhD research studentship and, finally, as an Assistant Professor lecturing about Football) and I add to this my practical experiences during the same period of time as fitness and assistant coach in many different football teams.

These influences have made me continuously reconsider previously learned skills, searching for richer ideas to present to football players during training sessions.

Referencing other authors is a risk as you may discriminate or forget other relevant influences, but three great ideologies have been used to form the basis of the training philosophy in this book.

The initial phase is closely related to gathering information about the bioenergetic or conditional performance component. It is possible that this primitive approach to the topic is unconsciously linked to the necessity of rationalising what happens inside the sport. Classic studies highlighting this approach have applied "Exercise Physiology" to football, as in the case of the research carried out by the Danish author Jens Bangsbo, or have used "Performance Analysis" (Bartlett, 2001) to integrate all the relevant information from the sport.

Many training systems have concluded their evolution in this primitive and pragmatic analysis stage. The phrase "football is an unscientific sport" has been attributed to Spanish coach Juanma Lillo. Without literally accepting this sentence, the application of the scientific method can help reduce the demagogy that often surrounds football training, it makes us remember the need to respect the unique and unrepeatable context that football represents.

Therefore, in order to bring light to its knowledge, the approach has to necessarily consider a variety of empirical sciences, from which the "General Theory of Systems" (proposed by Ludwig von Bertalanffy in the first half of the 20th century) appears to be especially relevant. Fortunately, these kinds of notions have started to be incorporated in the Sport Sciences Faculties. Javier Sampedro, a Professor in the Technical University of Madrid was one of the first lecturers to study team sports complexity under a praxiological (the study of human conduct) approach, where the essence is not the isolated sportsman's behaviour, but is instead inside the action of play ("acción de juego",

after Mahlo, 1969). From a practical point of view, Paco Seirul·lo can be considered as one of the first fitness coaches who broke with the traditional thinking line based on copying the contents used in individual sports and developed a different conceptual foundation to team sports training.

The ideological trilogy is momentarily closed, as it is a process in continuous evolution, with the ideas extracted from the intellectual movement generated in the Sport Sciences Faculty of Porto (Portugal), where its greatest exponent is Professor Vítor Frade. This transgressor line is sustained in systematic thinking (Tamarit, 2007) to produce a qualitative jump in the training methodology applied to football, in which the playing model of the team is the referential axis of the process.

Therefore, the Latin locution "citius, altius, fortius" (faster, taller, stronger), used by the Baron Pierre de Coubertin in the opening ceremony of the first modern Olympic Games is out of date when thinking about the full requirements that elite football players must possess in modern times.

The integration of all these thoughts shows an evolution in football training where fitness or conditioning can no longer be understood as a self-contained compartment but as an ecological and variable area which we must investigate to try and provide the best solutions to the problems that arise when playing the game. For instance, fitness should be trained specifically for playing football and never be treated independently from the game.

Football Specific Fitness Training

As soon as fitness is separated from the game it loses all its value. In certain occasions, the terminology has led to mistakes and the physical component of performance has been solely identified with off-the-ball activities. If we are beyond the philosophical debate between body and soul duality, it should be the same for the football player.

A footballer is a functional unit that behaves as a whole, so his performance cannot be split into independent plots. The classic training formula which includes an initial physical component, followed by a technical drill and concluding the session with a small sided game seems obsolete in relation to the holistic perspective that the process actually demands.

This substantial change requires fitness coaches to have a profound knowledge of the game, as all the training tasks proposed in a session have to come together in a common way of thinking sheltered in the team (tactical organisation). It may be possible that in the following years the term fitness coach will lose all its value and will no longer be used in the same way, simply being replaced by coach or assistant coach.

Taking these new training ideas into account, the traditional fitness coach has two different pathways; link his role to on the pitch matters as an additional member of the management staff or direct his responsibilities to off-the-field situations, more related with the medical staff.

On the Field Training or Gym Training?

Management Staff or Medical Staff?

Each professional needs to make his own decision depending on the role he wants to assume in the team.

Speed, Reactions and Tactical Intelligence

If a coach commits to study football there are always two variables that sooner or later appear: space and time. When progressing in the standard of competition the space and time for players to act is reduced. Therefore, it is not strange that speed represents a fundamental capacity in elite football as it relates to both variables. Each footballer has an acting speed but this velocity cannot be solely interpreted from a mechanical perspective as it requires a global approach. There are numerous examples of players that have compensated their conditional weaknesses with a faster resolution of gamerelated problems, developing what is known as *tactical intelligence*.

In the medium to long term, each player finds a level of competition where their speed of action allows them to be efficient. In a certain way, it is similar to what happens in motor sport; only those who can drive their cars faster can take part in Formula One races. The relationship between space and time is

also critical for coaches when designing their training sessions. Is it better to do a 6 v 6 possession drill in half or in a quarter of the field? Is it more effective to play a small sided game for 12 or 18 minutes? The answers to these kind of questions will always be specific to the training objectives and specific plans of the coach. The same training content can have a different effect depending on the space employed and its duration.

What Is the Right Way?

The aim of this book is to raise questions rather than provide a complete solution. Each coach has to think for themselves when faced with a blank sheet of paper or screen when ready to design their training sessions. There are no conclusive responses for each situation and football history lets us remember managers that have sustained success using many different methods.

There are managers that have achieved success trying to score more goals than their rivals and others who have been more concerned about not conceding as many goals as their opponent. As a matter of fact, what has been proved effective in one team might not be valid for another or, moreover, two teams treated the same way by different coaches during two consecutive seasons may not actually achieve the same results. This may read discouragingly, but it should represent a challenge and a hope for coaches. If this were not the case, coaches could be replaced by computers, which are more efficient. Fortunately, the interpersonal relationships being established during the training process become a qualitative factor in the final team performance and prevent computers from leading the operations.

What Will I Learn from This Book?

Throughout the book the reader is invited to a continuous thought about football´s training process, to enrich their experience. One of the aims of the book is to develop a methodological organisation of training. In chess (the greatest strategic sport) grandmasters are characterised by thinking many plays in advance of the actual situation.

Football training should aid to predict team performance in competition, limiting the effect of uncertainty (opponents, playing surface, crowd,

referees, luck, etc.). This demands high creative doses from coaches to be able to propose tasks which favour players learning about the game and develop an autonomous thinking to solve the problems that arise during the competition.

At the end, when space and time are limited, the one who finds a solution that nobody had come up with before is the one winning the game.

CHAPTER 1

THE ORGANISATION OF THE TRAINING PROCESS

1.1 THE COACH: DECISION MAKING FOR RELEVANT TEAM PERFORMANCE ISSUES

When beginning the duty of managing a football team there are many questions that need to be precisely defined. One of these preliminary matters is to identify what it is required to achieve with the team. The immediate response is usually an emphatic one: to win. Some audacious coaches can add a connotation: to win playing "good" football. The fact that success is often related with the final competition outcome makes coaches live in a permanent barbed wire, because winning can be influenced by a variety of factors.

Since football is a sport in which chance plays a very important role there are times where a team can win a match having performed worse than their opponents. For instance, winning a game is an isolated fact; what is really important for a coach is to be able to develop a playing model/style which helps to arrange and organise the behaviours of footballers on the field and enhances the possibility of winning a greater number of matches. This playing idea has to theoretically reflect all the essential aspects that characterise the team organisation and should be absorbed by all the players in the search for collective success.

This way intends to "operationalise" (after Mourinho, in Oliveira et al., 2007) the required behaviours in each of the four phases of the game: attack, defence, the transition from attack to defence and the transition from defence to attack. Even though this idea has to be dynamic and adaptable to the players´ characteristics and their evolution during the season, it represents a declaration of intent to embody the group identity on the field. The playing model can be broken up into a series of principles and sub-principles to facilitate the development of training strategies (Frade, in Diaz, 2012).

As an example, Figure 1 (on the next page) outlines the basic features of a Spanish professional team during the 2008-2009 season. This pattern was developed alongside the team manager, Abraham Garcia, in order to summarise the basic concepts that should govern the tactical functioning of the team.

The initial step for this model was to establish the theoretical organisation when the team had or didn't have the ball, and the actions to be done when possession was gained or lost. Each of the phases of the game were further divided into a series of categories according to the attacking type (positional or combinative, direct or with long balls, re-starts of play after corner kicks, indirect/direct free kicks, throw ins, etc.), the transition phase (attack -> defence and defence -> attack) and the defensive phase (with the reverse reasoning as before).

After dividing the game into these phases the principles and sub-principles which should rule the team´s collective behaviour were put forward. These kind of theoretical plans are only a static reconstruction of reality. The complexity of the problem is much greater when the ball and the footballers are moving. For instance, the playing models must be subjected to a permanent feedback process to so they can adapt successfully. During a season a team always evolves in a continuous way because of the individual player's and their opponent's participation impacts directly on the collective performance of the team.

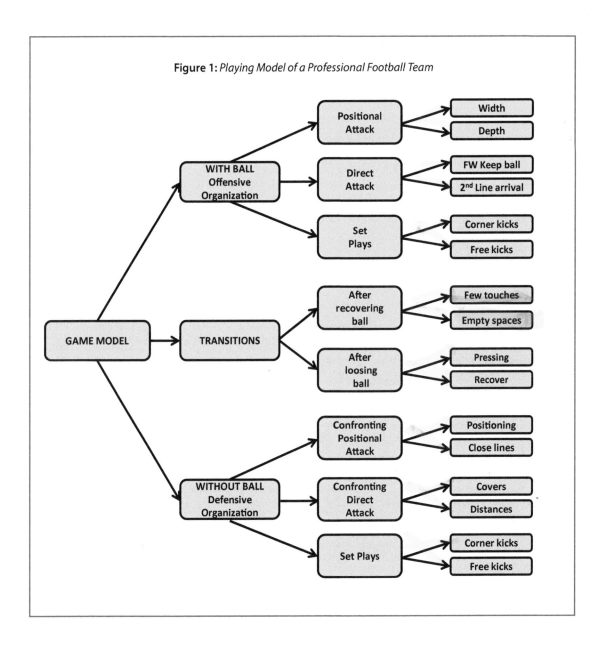

Figure 1: *Playing Model of a Professional Football Team*

To make it easier to understand this concept, Figure 1 only shows two fundamental ideas in each of the categories. It is clear that there are more principles that rule the organisation of each team, as Cano (2009) precisely reported in his analysis from F.C. Barcelona. Considering the attacking phase, the coach usually selects a priority direction, although having different alternatives enriches the team´s tactical culture and helps when responding to unexpected situations that might occur during competition.

For this reason, some of the principles from Figure 1 can be applied in more than one category. Moving the ball quickly with few touches, the movement of teammates to create space and provide options to the ball carrier, playing passes into empty spaces instead of to a teammates' feet, creating width, third-man runs, full back's overlapping runs, dribbling the ball forward to break the first line of pressure, having different ways of finishing including shooting from outside the penalty area, etc. are key aspects to achieve good attacking play.

The same procedure can be followed for the defensive phase, which can be characterised by occupying a fast and correct position when the ball is won by the opponent, advanced players pressing after losing possession, closing the passing lanes so the attackers have to move into less dangerous areas, adequate positioning for frontal and diagonal balls into the penalty box, marking players in the penalty area from crosses, quick and coordinated movements after the ball is cleared, the correct use of the offside rule, etc.

Once the coach has outlined all the basic principles that must rule the collective behaviour in each of the four phases of the game, these can be further subdivided into minor categories: sub-principles, subprinciples of the sub-principles, etc. (Mourinho, in Oliveira et al., 2007).

The final aim is to clearly identify all the collective conducts which need to be developed. Thereafter, training sessions can be designed to facilitate the occurrence of selected behaviours. As an example, if a coach wants to improve a defensive principle of a centre back covering the space behind the full back,

a methodological progression could be created for the teaching and learning process. The first of the tasks could be a situation where 3 attackers confront 2 defenders in a small space drill and have to reach an end zone. From this simple structure new elements can be added: 4 attackers, 3 defenders, goalkeepers, specific defending areas, etc. Hence, by learning from discovery, significant situations can be designed to help the footballer find out and incorporate the basic playing principles (Ruiz Perez, 1994).

In any case, writing down on paper the necessary skills to identity a team must have is a relatively easy task for any licensed coach. The huge leap forward is represented by those coaches that are able to properly teach their theoretical plans. It is here where the differences between coaches and those who line-up footballers can be most appreciated. It is not enough to just know who the best players in the team are, which is essential anyway, as it is also necessary to structure the players into a cooperative team for different situations that may occur during a match.

This can be achieved by defining a training style or defining the process to help obtain the expected results. This training philosophy should embrace the management of interpersonal relationships between the coach and players both on and off the field contributing to implement a working methodology that leads each player to identify the team playing model as their own. Team management at elite standard represents one of the greatest challenges for coaches because footballers often have disproportionate egos which compromise the objective of searching for a functional unit.

Many studies over the last years have reported that emotion is a very important catalyst (Damasio, 2005; Punset, 2010). These studies, based on emotional intelligence, can provide valuable information for coaches to help manage groups of players in order to establish strategies that attract the footballer towards training, while isolating the multiple external factors that usually damage their mental health. To be able to approach a training session with a positive attitude the footballer needs to recover the original pleasure for the game and the desire to learn and improve

throughout training. Once the footballer develops an emotional control and the ability to liberate the mind, it will be easier for him to be creative on the pitch. Furthermore, learning how to socially interact can be very useful for players to help them adopt emphatic and cooperative conducts with their teammates (Punset, 2011). Whatever the case, this topic requires a very meticulous analysis which goes beyond the aims of this book.

Even though a coach can clearly define their playing model and training style, there are a series of factors that might influence the final outcome. Without doubt, the level of the players that form the team has the greatest relevance, as the raw material has a decisive effect on the quality of the work.

The ideal situation is for the coach to have total control of what players he has in the team, hopefully based on his playing and training style, however in most cases this is not possible. When analysing the evolution of the sport during the last few decades, it can be seen that the criteria used to select a footballer has changed.

It is possible that the first qualitative jump was represented by the "pressing football" revolutionary vision of **Rinus Michels** (Batty, 1980). Some years later this idea was improved and introduced in Spain by **Johan Cruyff**, where all the players were involved in the attacking and defensive collective tasks and all the technical activities had to be executed at a high speed.

In the late 1980's **Arrigo Sacchi** added another crucial component to his teams: Tactical Organisation (Accame, 1995). The development of zone marking systems and pressing the opponent to reduce space and time to function caused players to speed up their cognitive processes as they had to respond to problems posed by opponents with a considerable time limitation. The most prestigious managers of the modern era have optimised those previous advancements and have added an extremely competitive character which is maintained during long periods, as the heavy fixture schedule demands.

The traditional preparation phase has gradually disappeared and competition appears from the initial training cycles to the end of the season. Taking all this into account it is not surprising that every coach wants players in their team with all these components: speed, technique, tactical intelligence and competitiveness. These are fundamental criteria when recruiting young players for the academies of football clubs.

In addition to the squad of players there are other issues which might impact the system. Building a management/coaching staff where all the members share and respect an identical working philosophy structured upon the team playing model is essential. The separation of tasks during the session, e.g. the fitness coach responsible for the offthe- ball activities and the coach for introducing ball-related contents is nowadays obsolete. The situation requests a more transversal perspective where all the coaches have to act in coordination during the session, transmitting clear messages to the players. To accomplish this purpose the manager must surround himself with qualified and pro-active staff (Espar, 2010) as this will make sure there is an improvement in training quality and will increase the chances for management and team success.

Communication strategies with all the other supporting staff of the club must also be defined. As football has become a global industry, clubs have incorporated more personnel with different duties which have created more complex communication networks. Two common conflictive areas for coaches are the Direction of Football (Football Operations) and the Medical Department, especially when the responsibilities for each area are not previously defined. The ability to solve conflicts has been identified by Punset (2011) as one of the key factors to survive in the 21st century. For instance, there must be an adequate hierarchy in the final decision making process to avoid conflicts of interest. The sooner these major lines of action are identified the better it will be in order to avoid misunderstandings.

Material facilities of the club (training ground, football pitches, gym, clinic, transportation, hotels, etc.) must be inventoried and be for the collective benefit. Furthermore, the social economic background of the

club has to be known. It is a reality in professional football that the demand for results often precedes the process being built to achieve it. Thus, if a coach wants to implement a long-term training philosophy in a club with a great social pressure and urgency for results, he needs to quickly adapt to the early demands if he wants to avoid being fired. Therefore, sometimes it is not worth accepting a job proposal without the minimum requirements to meet the objectives. Finally, cultural aspects can also limit the application of certain playing models. Each club, and its supporters, has characteristic football features which need to be acknowledged to avoid compromising the application of a playing idea.

Figure 2 outlines the initial decision making process of a coach in relation to the most relevant aspects that can affect football training. The greater the power the coach has in this decision making process the bigger the guarantees to manage the team according to his ideas will be. The paradigm of this representation could be the traditional English model where the manager had the power to decide upon all the essential aspects surrounding the club's management. As coaches have shared their power in the organisation of clubs, their decision making responsibility has decreased almost as much as their job stability. They are now usually the first person to leave when the demanded results on the field are not achieved.

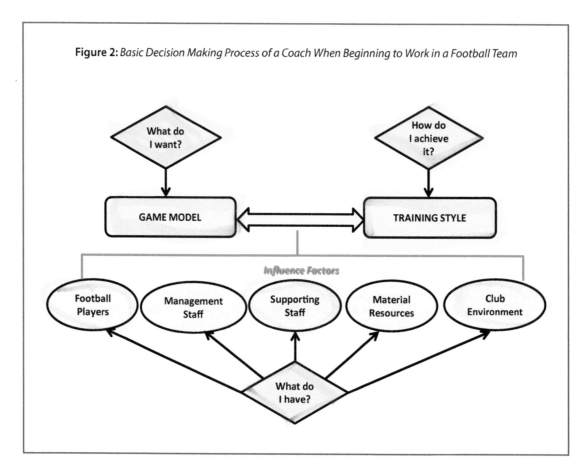

Figure 2: *Basic Decision Making Process of a Coach When Beginning to Work in a Football Team*

1.2 TRAINING STRUCTURE AND INJURY PREVENTION

On the basis of the ideas outlined in the previous section, two tools seem extremely important for coaches:

1. The capacity to design a playing model that optimises the characteristics of the squad.
2. The ability to develop a training style that enables you to achieve the maximum collective performance in competition.

At the same time, this training style has to combine the way to manage off (interpersonal relationships) and on-the-field issues. As each of these concepts permits deeper analysis, this book is only focused on the latter aim (on-the-field training methodology) thinking of football training as a dynamic and ecological system where there is a continuous interaction with the environment. The proposals are not unique and irreversible, so they need to be permanently adjusted depending on individual situations. By doing so, the system evolves and is cemented by the interrelationships emerged between the players.

The starting point of this process lies in establishing two clearly differentiated dimensions:

1. Collective training of the team.
2. Individual training of the footballers.
   (Figure 3 - Next Page)

Traditionally, the training of the players has followed a reductionist conception, based on isolating performance components, treating them independently and searching for a final summary of the effects.

However this should not happen in football as the whole is greater than the sum of its parts, so when eleven players take part in a team, this exponentially increases the complexity of the interaction network during the playing action (Sampedro, 1999). For this reason, the essence of the training process has to be structured around the collective aspects of the team organisation.

Each training session has to emerge from a number of tactical objectives which need to be reached, with principles and subprinciples (Mourinho, in Oliveira et al., 2007) and combined with a dynamic of the efforts; longer or shorter, with more or less recovery periods, depending on the day of the week or the month of the season the team is in.

There is not a standard rule which limits the duration of a training session. Coaches must develop an acute observation capacity to determine in which moment the proposed tasks are no longer effective to reach the objectives. Training times and energy expended should be optimised, looking for possible.

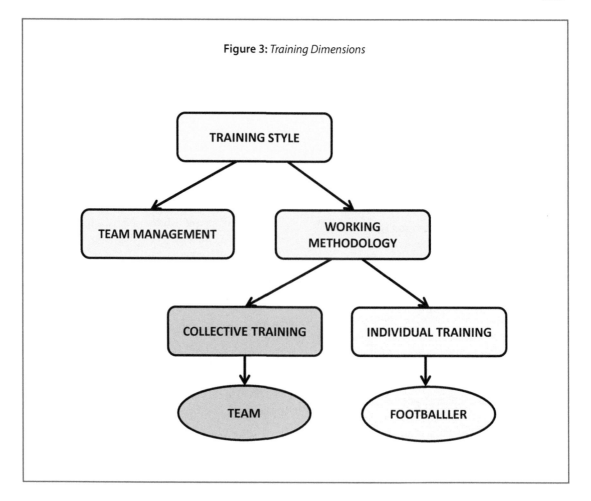

Figure 3: *Training Dimensions*

Individual training of a footballer cannot be understood as an end in itself, as the final aim has to be to integrate the performance of every player into the team. This notion is crucial not to disrupt the process direction.

Training in an individual way would take a club down the wrong pathway. Training grounds would end up being sport facilities for selected guests and activities such as Yoga or Pilates and the importance of the game itself will be forgotten. As Seirul·lo wisely indicates (in Pol, 2011), these complimentary activities can be beneficial for the players´ health, but using these training methods out of context does not equal an improvement in football capacities.

Accordingly, this individual training has an independent entity and can be carried out before or after the main team training sessions.

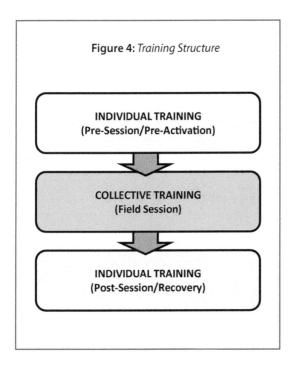

Figure 4: *Training Structure*

INDIVIDUAL TRAINING
(Pre-Session/Pre-Activation)

COLLECTIVE TRAINING
(Field Session)

INDIVIDUAL TRAINING
(Post-Session/Recovery)

Pre-training activities have the aim of preparing the footballer for the session and, in some cases, have also been called preactivations. They should be between 15 to 30 minutes long and never lead to a development of fatigue, as they present the opposite purpose. The contents should be based on a detailed examination of the individual requirements of each player, in which quality takes precedence over quantity in the executions.

It is essential for a coach to have the highest number of fit footballers for every competitive match, as this availability favours the management of resources and increases chances of success. The introduction of individual injury prevention programs is an important aspect to consider in this pre-training routine, always respecting the peculiarity of the sport. Occasionally, an excessive approach to preventive tasks can mean losing sight of the principal aim, which is the need for players to compete.

Football is a performance sport and at toplevel standard the players have to reach the highest demands. For instance, it is important to adjust the balance between performance and health. Having a good injury record would be no good if the team is not able to adequately perform in competition. However, an extremely low injury level can be due to excellent preventive work, although it could be questioned if the players have been far away from their adaptation potential limit. Again, a continuous deliberation is needed to maximise these theoretical performance thresholds without increasing the risk of injury to the players.

Research carried out with professional Swedish footballers has revealed that those players who had previous hamstring, groin and knee injuries were twice or three times more likely to sustain the same kind of injury during the next season (Hägglund et al., 2006).

Therefore, a detailed medical history of each player, together with a functional exploration can provide valuable data to help prescribe individual preventive exercise plans. Thus, aspects such as joint stability and mobility (principally in the ankle, knee and hip joints for outfield players), footprint alterations, landing mechanics, leg-length differences, pelvis position in relation to the transversal axis, lack of strength in the lumbar or abdominal muscles etc. might require special treatment to avoid future injuries.

The Risk of Injury

In addition to the individual risk (due to the medical history and bio-mechanical characteristics) there is a risk to the team associated to practicing football. The adoption of a consensus statement on injury definitions and data collection by the Fédération Internationale de Football Association Medical Assessment and Research Centre (Hägglund et al., 2005; Fuller et al., 2006) has led to the publication of a variety of studies during the last years. These investigations have determined that football players who took part in the UEFA Champions League had an average of 9.4 injuries every 1000 hours of exposure (Waldén et al., 2005). The risk of sustaining an injury during a game was higher than during training (30.5 v 5.8 injuries per 1000 hours, respectively; Walden et al., 2005).

To date, it cannot be concluded that there is a unique cause of injuries as these can be effected by previous injuries (Hägglund et al., 2006), the playing surface (Ekstrand et al., 2006), competition region (Hägglund et al., 2005; Waldén et al., 2005; Eirale et al., 2012), match density (Ekstrand, 2008; Dupont et al., 2010; Dvorak et al., 2011) and even the positional role of the player in the team formation (Dadebo et al., 2004; Fuller et al., 2004; Morgan & Oberlander, 2004; Woods et al., 2004) or how far the team is into the season might also have an effect (Waldén et al., 2005; Ekstrand et al., 2011).

In personal studies carried out during the last few years in the Spanish second division, footballers have shown that the overall injury risk was very similar to that of topflight footballers (9.3 injuries per 1000 hours), although injuries were 10 times more likely to occur in matches than during training (Mallo et al., 2011; Mallo & Dellal, 2012).

As the risk of incurring an injury appears to be similar at different levels, it seems essential to examine their frequency in relation to the days of absence from training (San Román, 2003). In this sense, the standard of the competition might have an effect on this variable as the number of days of absence was 30% higher in Spanish Division One footballers (909 days of absence per team per season; Noya & Sillero, 2012) than in those competing in Division Two (704 days of absence per team per season; Mallo, 2012a).

Similarly, injury severity could also be related to the competition standard as moderate episodes (absences between 8 and 28 days) were more frequent in the UEFA Champions League (Waldén et al., 2005) than in the Spanish third division. This was 2.8 v 2.3 per 1000 hours of exposure, respectively (Mallo, 2012a).

Additionally, this risk was almost three fold (1.4 v 0.5 injuries per 1000 hours) when comparing major injuries (more than 28 days absence) between these two standards (Waldén et al., 2005; Mallo et al., 2012a).

Injury Preventive Work Strategy

Once the individual and team risks have been estimated, it is necessary to implement a preventive work strategy to reduce the occurrence of these episodes. Muscle injuries located in the posterior side of the thigh have been reported as the most frequent in footballers (Waldén et al., 2005; Ekstrand et al., 2011; Mallo et al., 2012a; Noya & Sillero, 2012) and therefore require prophylactic measures in an attempt to decrease their incidence. Several studies have shown how focusing on strength improvements can reduce the risk of incurring this kind of injury (Askling et al., 2003; Mjolnes et al., 2004; Árnason et al., 2008).

There is a great variety of methods that can elicit deep hamstrings contractions, evolving from exercises without auxiliary equipment (like the "Nordics"; Mjolnes et al., 2004), to the use of exercise balls, balance boards or more complex inertial systems such as the "yo-yo" machines (Askling et al., 2003). The contents have to be carefully selected after a thorough examination of every particular case, adapting the exercises to the requirements of each player and always ensuring a correct technical execution.

As previously indicated, quality should be placed above quantity as we do not want players to be fatigued which can then compromise their match performance. Glute activation can also help reduce the risk of hamstring injuries. This is a big muscle group which, due to the daily sedentary activity, remains "un-switched" during long periods of time. Its activation in the pre-training phase can produce better hamstring efficiency.

It is important to add that improvement of flexibility in the posterior thigh muscles has also been reported as an effective tool to reduce their injury risk (Witvrouw et al., 2003).

Hip adductor muscles have also shown a high injury incidence in footballers (Ekstrand et al., 2011; Mallo et al., 2012a) and might benefit from specific treatment. Again, supervised contents that induce deep stretching (contractions) as in assisted exercises, exercise balls, balance boards, conic pulleys, etc. can help reduce this kind of injury.

Strength and torque imbalances in the pelvic region can be related to adductor-related groin pain, which can require long periods of absence from competition.

The combination of strength and coordinative exercises for the muscles surrounding the pelvis region has proven effective to prevent this type of injury (Holmich et al., 1999).

Triceps and quadriceps muscles complete the location of the most frequent muscle injuries in football players (Ekstrand et al., 2011). Noya & Sillero (2012) reported a very important finding regarding the recto femoris, as they found that injury in this muscle was most prominent with the highest absence rates in Spanish professional teams. Therefore, this muscle (which has an action in both the hip and knee joints) requires a special consideration when prescribing preventive programs as it is continuously used in typical game actions such as kicking, jumping or to decelerate and change direction.

Joint Mobility

In addition to muscle injuries, joint pathology also has a big impact on the availability of players for competition (Waldén et al., 2005; Mallo et al., 2012a; Noya & Sillero, 2012). Without taking into consideration direct trauma injuries which are difficult to avoid due to the nature of the sport itself, the strengthening of joint periphery muscles and sensitive perceptual motor education (with the inclusion of pro-prioceptive exercises) has been shown to be effective to prevent ankle and knee injuries (Caraffa et al., 1996; Junge et al., 2002) resulting in a 50% lower risk of football players sustaining ankle sprains during the last few years (Ekstrand, 2008).

Strength Training

Exercises oriented to improve different strength capacities in the players can also be used in this pre-training session time. In this case, strength training has to follow a functional approach directed to the application of forces under sport-specific movements and never focused on developing strength in muscles by themselves. Thus, classical body-building exercises using weight machines and prolonged concentric abdominal sets (the traditional "crunches") do not seem to be the best strength training for footballers.

The exercises must respect football activity patterns and the available time to apply the force inside the sport. Altogether, exercises focused on single-leg supports, intra and inter-muscle coordination and pillar strength (Athletes Performance, 2011) may be particularly relevant. These contents have to be adjusted to the motor competence of each player, establishing individual methodological progressions.

The correct bio-mechanical execution must be secured during the exercise, with a neutral lumbar-spine position and force vectors directed in the adequate directions, including not only linear movements but also rotational strength manifestations, in the same way as they occur during the sport. Under this heading, high speed and short duration exercises, as classical low impact plyometrics, could also be included in the program as neuromuscular pre-activations.

Mental Training

Even though the great majority of pre-team training activities are focused on the conditional component, introducing psychological (mental training) or technicaltactical content should not be overlooked. In this case, pre-activation would be linked to the cognitive component. The use of audiovisual media can ease the transition to on-the-field situations, with an aim of achieving a feed forward effect towards the following training practices.

Recovery

Training to be carried out at the end of the training session has a close connection to that preceding it, although in this case the purpose is accelerating the recovery processes.

Performance can be theoretically broken down into training effects and fatigue caused. If training effects are high but there is also an elevated fatigue, the player will have a small margin of progression and will experience difficulties to perform at his best the following day. Therefore, both aspects must be combined, in order to achieve the greatest effects with the lowest accumulated fatigue.

This post-session phase can include complementary

strength exercises as well as stretching and flexibility routines, although the main part of this period has to be occupied by physiotherapy, principally by manual therapy. All the shortened and damaged soft tissue structures need to be treated so the player confronts the next training session in an optimal physical status.

Adding hydrotherapy (ice baths, contrasts) to the previous content can be an auxiliary method to fulfil this process. Ensuring the adequate fluids and nutrients replacement after training is another fundamental aim.

The use of supplements and ergogenic aids (any external influences that can be determined to enhance performance in highintensity exercises) can help optimise the recovery processes and prevent deficiency states.

Tactical Analysis

Tactical analysis cannot be ignored at the end of training. In this case, the aim will be to evaluate the activity with a feedback effect. Again, the use of video analysis systems can be a valuable tool to help the players learn the contents, with adapted explanations to the individual learning pace of each person.

Finally, psychological training can also play an important role at the end of the collective session.

CHAPTER 2

THE COLLECTIVE
TRAINING SESSION

THE COLLECTIVE TRAINING SESSION

With reference to the diagram shown in Figure 3, this Chapter aims to present a methodology to structure on field training in football. The way this has been done can be slightly different to other books with similar purposes, as in the present case the tactical organisation aspects are intended to be linked with those related to the dynamic of the efforts (which are traditionally more related with the fitness coach). For instance, the holistic training ideas shown in the previous pages are respected, enhancing the fact that all the members of the management staff need to share common ideas.

The collective field session is the training nucleus as it represents the "homework" that players have to do in order the reach the "exam" (match) with a broad range of creative responses to solve all kinds of problems that could emerge during competition.

Referring to a collective session does not necessarily mean that all the players have to receive the same kind of stimulus, but the stimulus should be oriented in the same direction. For instance, the tasks should be designed based on the playing model of the team, from which the game principles and any other sub-category are established (Frade, in Diaz, 2012). The way to implement this can differ between coaches depending on their training style, since every coach has a particular vision of each drill and how to apply it to his players.

As previously indicated, there is more than one possibility to achieve objectives and, on the basis of the parameters of each situation, every coach can develop a multitude of variants in accordance with their creativity.

From all of the above, collective training has to integrate tasks for the essential team function aspects, which need to be chronologically sequenced in the three phases of the session (Figure 5) which will be expanded in the next sections.

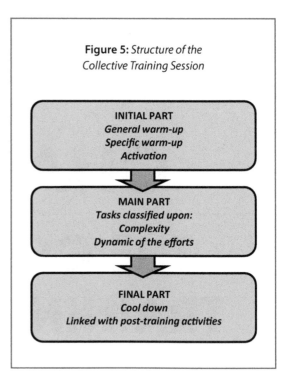

Figure 5: *Structure of the Collective Training Session*

INITIAL PART
General warm-up
Specific warm-up
Activation

MAIN PART
Tasks classified upon:
Complexity
Dynamic of the efforts

FINAL PART
Cool down
Linked with post-training activities

2.1 THE INITIAL PART OF THE SESSION

The start of any demanding physical activity must be preceded by a warm up. The warm up can be considered as a transition phase which has to respect where the player is coming from (home, physiotherapy, gym, any external job if he is not a professional footballer, etc.) and where they are going to (the fundamental part of the session).

The physiological benefits of the warm up have been detailed in a variety of texts, favouring a gradual adaptation from all the systems and organs to the effort at the same time of preventing the occurrence of injuries (Weineck, 1988). Care must be taken not to stay in this commitment level, as it is also necessary to achieve an adequate mental activation so the player can take advantage of the session right from the start of it. For this reason, the warm up should not be limited to conditional stimulus and sport-specific motor patterns, but should also be complemented with cognitive elements, introducing activities which request the solution of minor mental problems.

As it does not have an end in itself, the same kind of start to the session can always be employed. However, presenting an identical type of stimulus in this initial phase of the session can limit the adaptation potential of the players and, in a long term, the response will be less effective. To avoid this it seems interesting to change the warm ups so the players are fully alert in every session. On the other hand, this does not mean that you move to the opposite extreme. The warm up has to be preparatory and should not be an interference to the main part of the session.

The players´ education is essential to carry out varied and dynamic warm ups. If a team is used to performing very organised off-theball warm ups and one day the coach introduces a very creative warm up, it is possible that not all the players will be able to adapt correctly and the basic objectives of this phase will not be achieved. Thus, an adequate progression of the stimulus provided to the players is needed during the season. If the coach wants to have quick, technical and autonomous decision making players, all these qualities must be present in all parts of the session.

2.1.1 WARM UP PHASES

Figure 5 summarises three phases in which, theoretically, the initial part of the session can be divided into; general warm up, specific warm up and activation. This structure does not need to be strictly followed in all the training sessions, but it is a good way to organise the objectives to achieve. When taken to practice, these phase limits are often not so clear and certain contents can be used in more than one phase. The duration of each phase needs to be adjusted to the external constraints of each moment. An adverse weather situation may require a more structured and simple warm up and more favourable weather conditions can help introduce creative proposals. Nevertheless, each coach is the principal manager of the organisation of these contents which should always be similar to the tasks to be carried out in the main part of the session.

The general warm up aims to raise the response of all the systems (cardiovascular, respiratory) which are in charge of providing oxygen for the muscles and at the same time, of increasing the body temperature. This phase can include jogging, exercises for the major muscle groups, dynamic stretching and mobility exercises. Contents with the ball, performed at a low-intensity do not need to be necessarily excluded from this phase of the warm up. The overall duration should not be very long and even 5 minutes can be enough for top-class professional players, provided they are focused from the start of the session.

Specific warm ups is the second phase and, includes sport-specific motor patterns with and without the ball (changes of direction, jumps, accelerations, decelerations, etc.) which can be carried out with the interaction of teammates. The contents used in this phase have to keep a greater relation with the main part of the session, easing into the transition and optimising the effective training time.

Finally, the warm up can be concluded with a short activation which chains the initial and main parts of the session. The contents can be oriented towards the central nervous system, requesting cognitive responses during the activity. The volume of the stimulus cannot be high and a complete recovery between them must be secured, to avoid carrying fatigue to the next part of the session. Some of the tactical tasks that will be shown later in detail can be included in this phase, as long as the intensity is adapted to this earlier moment of the session.

Although each situation needs individual consideration, 15 minutes should be enough time for a warm up. You can also give 1-2 minutes for the players to hydrate and to carry out individual activities, as some players prefer doing their own routine of exercises during this initial phase. Unless there are justified causes, 25 to 30 minutes long warm ups can create an additional mental and physical fatigue to the player. It also limits the time for the main part of the session.

2.1.2 TYPES OF WARM UPS

All the players do not need to necessarily follow the same kind of warm up at the beginning of a session. If, as an example, during the main part of the session the midfielders and attackers are doing some crossing and finishing while the defenders are working on passing out from the back, all the players can start with a generic warm up and then progress into more specific routines and activations. The fitness coach does not have the exclusive property of the warm up and it is essential to have a collaboration between all members of the coaching staff. A warm up with the players divided into two groups of ten players supervised by two coaches can often offer more to the players than a unique warm up carried out by a single coach.

For the purpose of this book a simple classification of the types of warm ups has been established, taking a basic premise as a reference; if the ball is or is not used (Figure 6). After this classification, progressions can be developed to adapt the warm ups to the different initial phases. Furthermore, different types of warm ups can be combined in order to achieve the aims proposed.

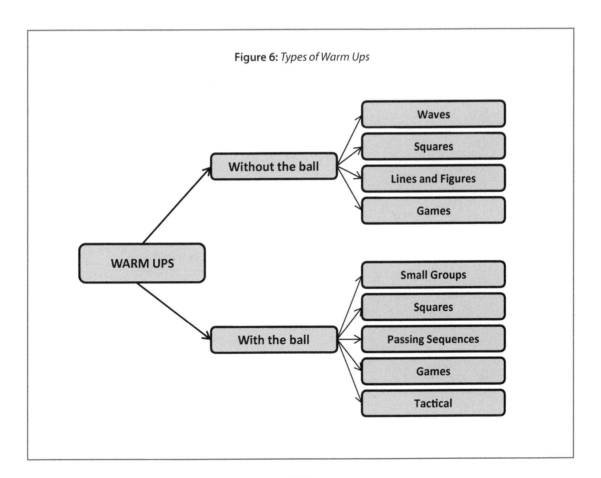

Figure 6: *Types of Warm Ups*

PRACTICE FORMAT

Each practice includes clear diagrams with supporting training notes such as:

- Name of Practice
- Objective of Practice
- Description of Practice
- Variation or Progression (if applicable)
- Coaching Points

KEY

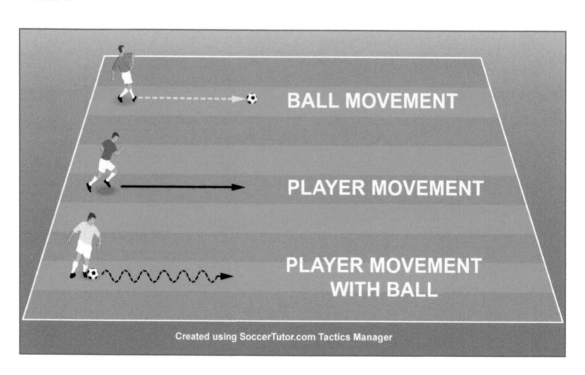

BALL MOVEMENT

PLAYER MOVEMENT

PLAYER MOVEMENT WITH BALL

Created using SoccerTutor.com Tactics Manager

WARMING UP WITHOUT THE BALL

Basic Warm Up - Running in 'Waves'

Created using SoccerTutor.com Tactics Manager

Objective

A warm up with general mobility exercises.

Description

This first exercise includes all the situations where the players move simultaneously in one direction. Vary the players movements with exercises such as normal jogging, running backwards, side-to-side, jumping up to head, etc.

It is a very basic type of warm up which can be carried out while moving around the field, from one penalty box to the other, using the width or half the length of the pitch.

Coaching Points

1. Include joint mobility exercises to open up the hips and shoulders in particular.
2. Make sure the players do their required stretches before, during or after this warm up exercise. Many players may have their own routine for this.

Basic Warm Up - Running in Squares

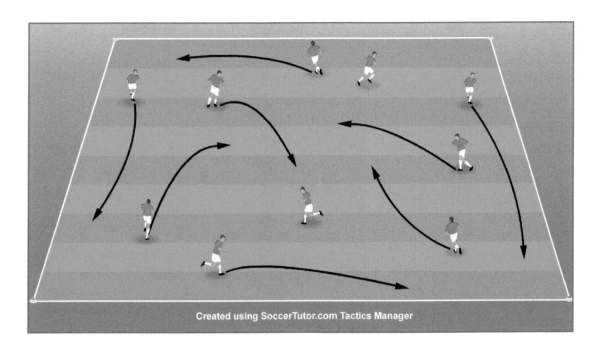

Created using SoccerTutor.com Tactics Manager

Objective

A warm up with general mobility exercises.

Description

This warm up is done within marked out squares. The size of the squares will depend upon the number of players. You can also group the players within different shapes such as rectangles, triangles or circles.

The difference to the previous warm up is that the players now move freely and with their own individually chosen trajectories inside the space, constantly changing direction.

Coaching Points

1. The players should use their run to attack the space.
2. Encourage the players to use changes of direction and different types of running i.e. side to- side running.
3. Make sure the players have their heads up and are aware of the players around them so they avoid collisions.

Changing Direction with Quick Feet in a Speed & Coordination Exercise

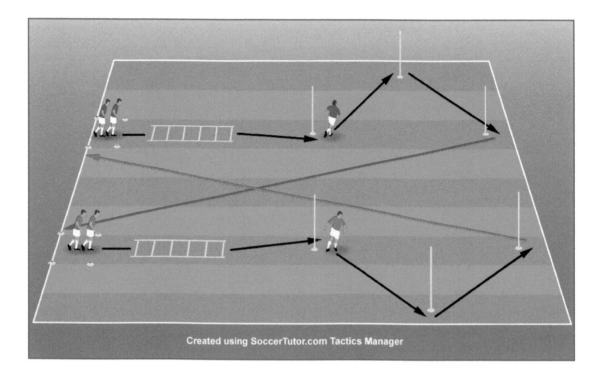

Created using SoccerTutor.com Tactics Manager

Objective

To warm up, develop coordination, explosive power and speed endurance/conditioning.

Description

The players are organised into 2 lines. The players perform a coordination exercise on the ladder, changes of direction through the poles and jog to the end of the opposite line.

Even though this is a simple exercise, you can use multiple variants by changing the sequence or adding additional elements such as speed rings and hurdles or add a ball so the players change direction whilst dribbling.

Coaching Points

1. Use varying techniques on the speed ladder such as 2 inside touches / 1 outside, 1 inside touch / 2 outside. Players need good rhythm and quick feet to accomplish the tasks.

2. To decelerate the players need to shorten their steps and bend their knees on the approach to the poles, before changing direction.

3. This exercise should start slowly (as this is a warm up) and the players can increase the speed as they go on. Monitor this closely.

Running & Switching Positions Tag Game

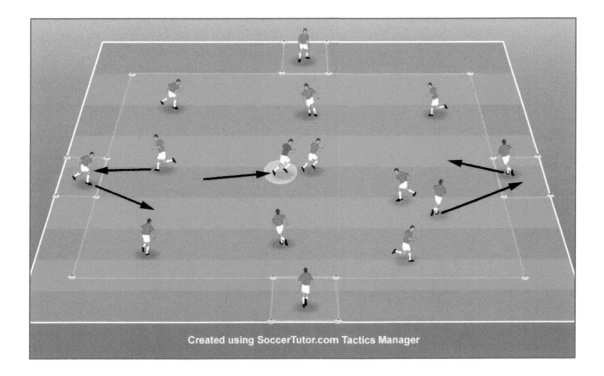

Created using SoccerTutor.com Tactics Manager

Objective

We work on speed, acceleration, reactions and awareness in a warm up exercise.

Description

The last of our warm ups without the ball shows an example of a game. This creates an activity with a recreational component and when it is used well, it can serve as a valuable catalyst and motivation for the players.

We mark out a large rectangle zone with a small square on each side as shown. There is 1 player in the main zone who has to try and 'tag' the other players, but is not allowed to tag the players who are in the small squares. Change the blue player often.

Only one player can be in the small squares at a time. If a second player goes to an outside square, the player who was there has to leave the square, as shown in the diagram.

Coaching Points

1. You can add an extra blue player to increase the intensity of the exercise.
2. Players should always be moving and constantly changing direction.
3. Awareness and reactions are key to the flow of the exercise and to avoid collisions.

WARMING UP
WITH THE BALL

Technical: Passing Combinations in Groups of 3

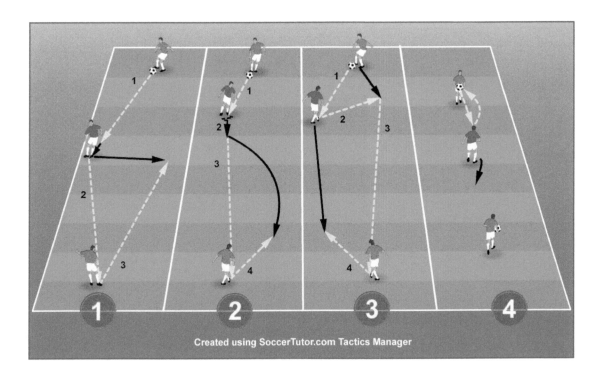

Created using SoccerTutor.com Tactics Manager

Description

GROUP 1: The player in the middle moves from side to side to receive the passes and simply plays the ball to each end continuously.

GROUP 2: The player in the middle now makes a movement to the end and offers a diagonal support angle to receive, controls the ball, turns and plays to the other end.

GROUP 3: The middle man (blue) moves from end to end and the red players play a 1-2 combination with him and then make a long pass to the opposite side themselves.

GROUP 4: The players are now closer and the red players hold the ball. They throw the ball up to the middle man who heads the ball back and turns 180° to face the other player.

Introducing the ball in a warm up does not increase the risk of injury. The relationship between the player and the ball is essential in football, so simple combinations or fundamental individual techniques can be used from the beginning of the session. It is also more motivational for the players and eases the transition to the main part of the session.

Coaching Points

1. Players should receive and pass with the back foot.
2. The middle player should already be half turned when receiving, letting the ball roll across their body.

Technical: Passing & Receiving Square

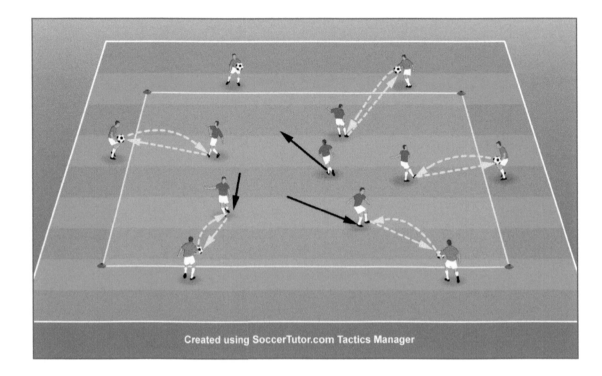

Created using SoccerTutor.com Tactics Manager

Objective

To develop passing and receiving on the ground and in the air during a warm up.

Description

In an area 20 x 15 yards, half the players have a ball in their hands outside the space and the other players are inside without a ball. The red players throw the ball to the red players who play the ball back, before moving to another outside player to do the same.

Change the roles often so players spend the same amount of time inside as outside.

Variations

1. Receive and pass back, 1 touch volley, head the ball back, 1 touch in the air and volley.
2. Players in the middle receive from the outside players, then dribble or juggle the ball to the next outside player and play the ball to them. They then move to receive from the next outside player.

Coaching Points

1. The inside players should be moving at all times.
2. The volleying and juggling aspects are useful to aid joint mobility.

40

Periodization Fitness Training

Passing 'Y' Shape Combination with Middle Man

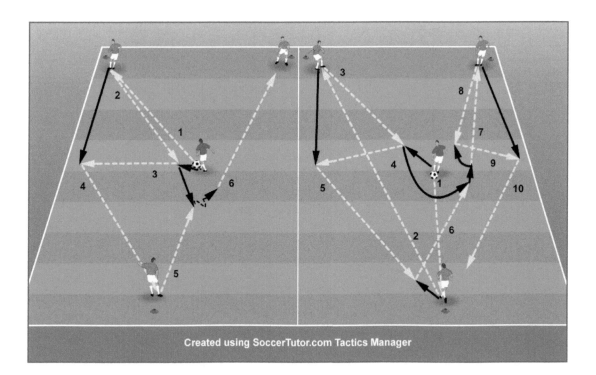

Objective

To improve short passing and timing of movement during a warm up.

Description

Divide the players into groups of 4 and position them in a 'Y' shape as shown with one middle player (blue). The ball is played from one side to the central man, who turns each time to a different side (pass and move). The sequence of the passes is shown by the numbers and the movement by the black arrows.

From this structure the number and difficulty of the passes can be increased. We have displayed a good example of this on the right hand side of the diagram.

Passing sequences, also known as technical figures, represent pre-established passing and moving combinations and can be an additional way to organise the warm ups with the ball.

Coaching Points

1. The players should pass and receive with the back foot (foot furthest away from the ball).
2. The weight and timing of the passes for the movement is key to the rhythm of the exercise.

Pairs Possession Exercise

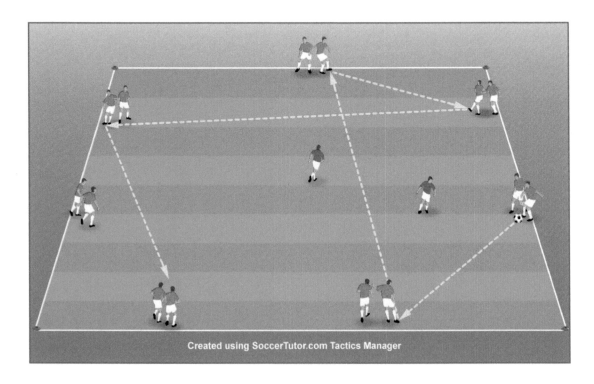

Created using SoccerTutor.com Tactics Manager

Objective

To develop passing, awareness of space, maintaining possession and pressing in a warm up.

Description

Mark out an area suitable for the amount of players. The players are in pairs and have to be holding hands. In the diagram example we have 7 pairs on the outside of the area keeping possession against 2 defenders (blue). The players in pairs are limited to 1 touch and the pair inside the space have to try to touch the ball.

Variations

Limit the players to 1 touch; same pair players cannot pass the ball between each other; players in the middle have to be holding hands, etc.

This is a recreational game which can motivate the group. These fun and activation components are beyond technical and tactical considerations.

Coaching Points

1. Use of the space: Utilise the full width with good mobility of the players on the outside.
2. Players need to coordinate with their partner to create the correct body position to play with 1 touch.

Tactical Shape and Building Up Play in a Warm Up Exercise

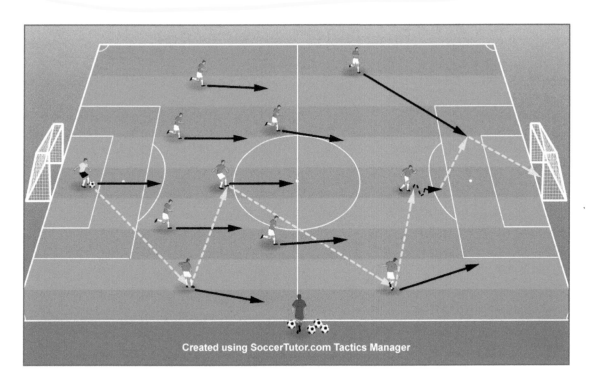

Created using SoccerTutor.com Tactics Manager

Objective

To develop tactical movements and passing in the possession phase (building up play) while warming up with general mobility exercises.

Description

The players start in the team formation on a full sized pitch (4-3-3 shown in diagram). To start, the coach blows the whistle and the players do warm-up exercises for 1 minute forwards and backwards (along a 10-15 yard imaginary lane) from their starting position.

After 1 minute, the coach blows the whistle again and the 11 players start moving the ball from their playing position as shown in the diagram. There is 1 ball for all of them and they have to pass and move, always from their specific position, finishing by scoring a goal.

After 1 minute, the coach blows the whistle again, they leave the ball, and they perform warm up exercises at a higher intensity this time. After 1 minute (we are now starting the 4th minute) the coach blows the whistle again and they do the pass and move element again.

Variations for the Warm Up without the Ball Phases

1. The forward leads the exercise and the other players have to do the same exercise as he does. When the forward turns, everybody has to turn back (as if the was going to press the ball).

2. Increase the intensity of the warm up exercise in each 1 minute phase.

Variations for the Warm Up with the Ball Phases

1. Use 2-3 balls so more players are actively involved.

2. The players always use 2 touches and should be constantly moving.

3. Not all the phases have to be 1 minute long and can be longer. Alternatively, you can do 1 minute without the ball + 2 minutes with the ball.

In this final exercise a tactical warm up has been introduced, which is very different from the previous ones as the activities carried out are based on the positioning of the players inside the team's formation. This type of warm up allows a quick transition to tactical drills or to the practice of set-plays. The coordination between the coaches is essential when introducing this type of warm up.

Coaching Points

1. The players should move collectively in relation to where the ball is.

2. The coach can stop the play to advise on the correct positioning, movement or passing.

2.2 THE MAIN PART OF THE SESSION

This part of the session has to be in line with the playing model of the team and the training style adopted, so it requires the active participation from all the members of the coaching staff. The aims are based on the tactical component and trying to work on football-specific situations in an attempt to encourage the decision making of the players and increase their knowledge of the game. At the same time, the training contents must be correctly judged to the length and intensity of the stimulus and to the stage of the season the team is in.

The practices represent the way to organise the activities in order to be able to achieve the objectives which were initially planned. At the same time, these practices are used to set up the direction of the teaching and learning process.

There is no doubt that the standard of the players has a huge impact on the selection of the practices. Hence, if the training is for young players who have just been introduced to the sport, the purposes should be adapted to their early development stage. Therefore, as an example, there is no sense looking into a playing formation for players aged 10-11 years old if they do not possess the essential capacities to combine their perception of space and time.

This book will focus on two basic parameters to classify the practices that are used in the main part of the session; complexity of the practices and how the dynamic of the efforts are distributed.

The Complexity of the Practices

This intends to reflect the relationship they have with resolving problems faced during game related scenarios. It is not simply about planning motor tasks which are difficult to execute for a footballer, as they should represent actions which are actually performed in competitive matches. As an example, a running drill in which a player has to perform a somersault and then shoot at goal can be difficult to carry out

for a footballer, but it is not a skill which occurs during a match. The complexity of this activity will be almost non-existent according to the categorisation employed in the actual chapter. In some cases, the term complexity could be related to specificity, although in others it could cause controversy.

Is it more specific for a full back to run by himself the length of the pitch and then cross a ball without any opposition or a within a small sided game with teammates and opposition?

These kinds of questions can lead to divergent answers, since the former is an analytical and closed proposal whereas the latter represents a global and open action, without respecting the playing position.

For the purpose of the actual classification, the small sided game will be more complex as it requires further adjustments in the decision making process of the player. Some coaches might consider it less specific than the previous one, but these kinds of tasks can be used as a foundation for learning activities related to the playing model of the team.

How the Dynamic of the Efforts Are Distributed

The second parameter employed to classify the tasks is how the dynamic of the efforts are distributed. Although, inside the sport, the word effort is normally associated with the physical component, in the actual context it covers all the dimensions of the player. This highlights the importance of managing all the variables in each practice; number of players taking part, space, duration (number of sets and repetitions and recovery periods between them) and rules, to try to establish and characterise a particular dynamic of the efforts.

A drill/practice can have a very different outcome just by changing one of these components; playing the offside rule in a 6v6 small sided game will certainly affect the pattern (cognitive, motor and metabolic).

2.2.1 THE COMPLEXITY OF THE PRACTICES

Table 1: *Summary of the 4 Levels of Complexity and their Fundamental Characteristics*

1. CONDITIONING	Practices without the ball and non-specific decision making.
2. TECHNICAL	With the ball specific motor coordination and non-specific decision making.
3. TACTICAL	The decision making process of the footballer is stimulated.
3a. Passing Exercises	The movement of the ball is prioritised over the movement of the players.
3b. Possession Exercises	The players and the ball move. Positional play is not included.
3c. Positional Practices	The players and the ball move, positional play and direction of play introduced (1-2 playing phases).
3d. Positional Games	The players and the ball move, positional play and directional games including all the phases with constraints.
4. COMPETITIVE	Few constraints. Application of principles modelled on competition.

2.2.2 THE COMPLEXITY OF THE PRACTICES; FIRST 3 LEVELS

The notion of complexity represents the difficulty or the grade of sophistication that a training drill/practice involves (Díaz Otañez, 1982; Bompa 1999) and it is closely associated to its cognitive demands. The role of Seirul·lo is especially relevant when addressing this topic as he has been one of the authors which has brought more light to the specific training aspects of team sports. Based on the studies carried out by this author (Seirul·lo, 1987, 1994, 2001) as well as by Solé (2002, 2006, 2008) and Roca (2011), four levels of complexity of the practices have been established in this book, where each of these levels contains the previous one. These levels can also be used to identify the development stages of young footballers. But, in order to achieve mastery of the ball, the body and of competition, it is essential to have personal emotional control. The psychological and social process lay behind any voluntary movement and, without controlling them, it is impossible to progress in the different dimensions of the game and within the evolution as a sportsman.

Figure 7: Levels of Approximation to the Complexity of Training Drills/Practices

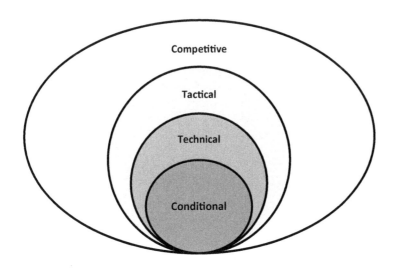

1. CONDITIONING

The first of the levels integrates all the tasks which are focused on this component and where no technical and tactical (specific decision making) behaviours are requested on the footballers. This group contains all the traditional without the ball fitness contents oriented to the bio-energetic performance component.

The exercises are not specific to football and could also be employed in other team sports with common physical demands, such as hockey or rugby. The only similarity comes, in some cases, by the intermittent pattern of the displacements. It is not a question of undermining these kinds of contents, but it is important to know the exact moments when to use them.

2. TECHNICAL

Level 2 (technical) includes situations designed towards the development of the individual or collective technique of the players. In this way, they are based in the execution mechanism, the motor coordination necessary to solve, in isolation, a match related problem. The fact that the aim is to develop or stimulate the specific coordinative patterns (skills) implies a qualitative difference with the warm ups with the ball, which presented the purpose of introducing the player to the session. Nevertheless, the same kind of contents could be employed in both cases as long as the methodological considerations which rule each part of the session are respected. As an example, a combinative drill in groups of three where all the players go through the three positions (crossing the ball to the penalty box or finishers trying to score) could be a technical task, as the technical requirements are taught outside of the playing position.

3. TACTICAL

The third level (tactical) tries to partially or totally reproduce match specific activities and the decision making process becomes the emphasis of the practice. As indicated in the previous chapter, the training process has to facilitate the consolidation of the team playing model, so this level should be the epicentre of the on the field training methodology. After work from several lecturers from the Sports Sciences Faculty of Porto (Portugal), the most prominent of them being professors Vítor Frade and Guilherme Oliveira, a new football training methodology has been developed and is known as Tactical Periodization (Tamarit, 2007).

One of the main characteristics of this new vision is the necessity to structure training on the basis of the way the coach wants his team to play (Rui Faria, in Campos, 2007). This implies that the conditioning and technical components are often considered out of context, whereas practices based on the principles and sub-principles which characterise the team playing concept are prioritised (Frade, in Díaz, 2012).

The training direction must be oriented towards specificity, with the practices including the four dimensions of football; physical, technical, tactical and psychological and the four phases of the play; attack, defence, the transition from defence to attack and the transition from attack to defence (Tamarit, 2007).

2.2.3 TACTICAL PRACTICES; 4 SUB-LEVELS

Continuing with the considerations from the previous pages and taking up the criteria of complexity, the tactical practices have been further divided into four sub-levels. This allows implementing teaching and learning progressions for each of the principles and sub-principles that form the playing model of the team.

A) Passing Exercises

More basic tactical concepts are employed and the practices prioritise the movement of the ball rather than the movement of the players. These tasks represent an advanced level to the traditional possession exercises, as rules to constrain the play are introduced.

A practical example could be a passing exercise with 10 players (3 teams of 3 players plus a neutral player) who play in a 20 x 10 yard rectangular space. Two of the teams are positioned outside the rectangle (2 players on each long side and 1 player on each short side). The neutral player provides support inside the space and the third team tries to win the ball. Please see the diagram below.

6 (+1) v 3 Passing Rectangle Exercise

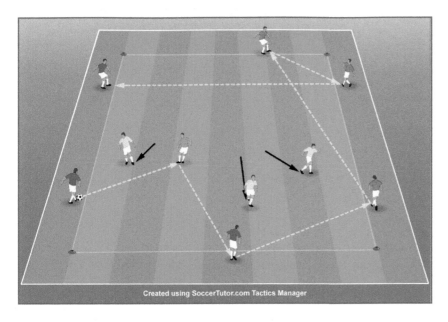

Created using SoccerTutor.com Tactics Manager

Variations

1. All the players are limited to 2 touches.
2. Outside players have 2 touches and the neutral player has 1 touch.
3. All the players are limited to 1 touch.

Change roles after a certain number of ball recoveries for a team.

Periodization Fitness Training

B) Possession Exercises

This category includes all the practices aimed at keeping the ball within spaces. In contrast to the passing exercises, where the movement of the ball was emphasised over the movement of the players, these practices must combine both factors; ball circulation and player movement (with a focus on creating space). This organisation allows us to work on more tactical principles.

The difference in relation to the next sub-level of complexity will be that the players do not respect their positional role in the team formation. An example of this kind of practice could be represented by an 8v8 possession game with no restrictions on movement, as shown below.

8 v 8 Possession Game

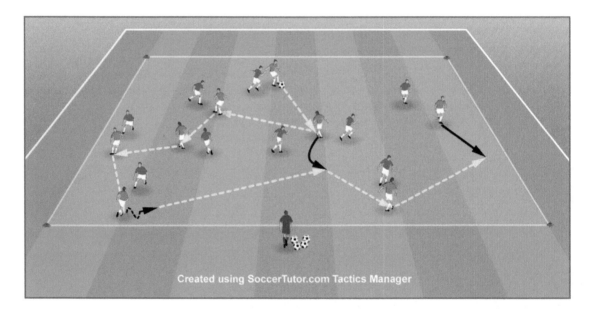

Created using SoccerTutor.com Tactics Manager

Description

The players play a free 8v8 possession game. The coach plays a new ball in immediately after the ball goes out of play.

Coaching Points

1. The correct angles and distances for support play are required and should be monitored.
2. At least 2 players need to provide an immediate passing option for the neutral player (left and right of him).

Periodization Fitness Training

C) Positional Practices

In this advanced approach the players start from their playing position and the activities are principally focused on one or two of the four phases of the game, working mainly in one direction. The four phases are attacking, defending, the transition from defence to attack and the transition from attack to defence.

The practices are focused on tactical concepts adapted to the specific positional role. To show you an example we have a situation below where 6 players (4 midfielders and 2 forwards) attack a back 4 of defenders plus a goalkeeper.

6 v 4 (+GK) Attack v Defence Practice

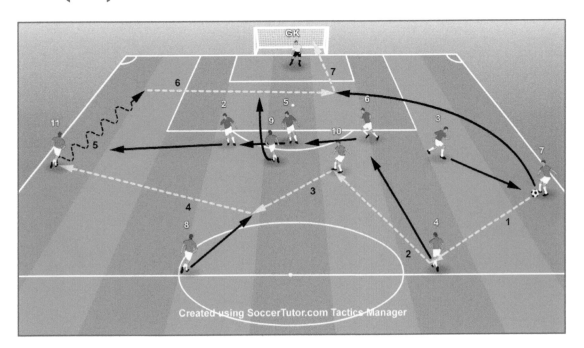

Description

We play 6v4 (+ GK) and the practice starts with the an attacking wide player (red) as that team try to find a solution to score.

The player's movements and positioning is key when working with teammates in a system of play. Monitor this and give instructions to the players when necessary.

Each sequence ends with a cross, shot on goal or if the ball goes out of play.

D) Positional Games

This final sub-level respects the position of the player and the activities can incorporate all four phases of the game. The elements that are used to differentiate this practice from the previous ones is the introduction of rules to organise the practice and to determine the way to score a goal. These ruled or constrained games work towards learning certain tactical principles.

The example shown is an 7v7 game where we respect the playing positions. A team scores a goal when they receive a pass in the "end zone" of the opposition team.

Position Specific 7 v 7 End Zone Small Sided Game

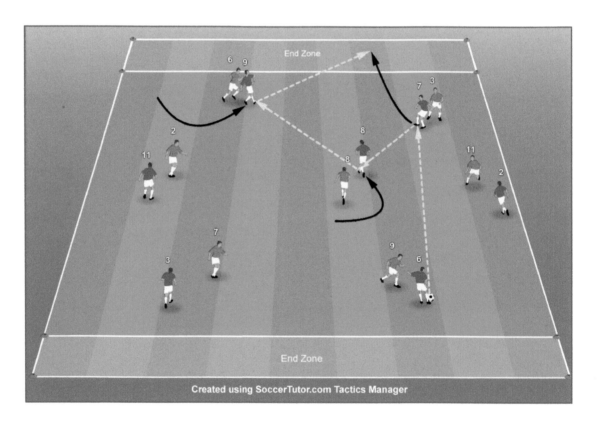

Description

We play a 7v7 small sided game with 2 end zones. Both teams are in a 3-3-1 formation and respect their positions. Each team has 3 defenders, 3 midfielders and 1 forward.

A goal is scored when the ball is received within an 'end zone' successfully.

2.2.4 THE FINAL LEVEL OF COMPLEXITY; COMPETITIVE

The fourth and last level of complexity (competitive) is narrowly linked to the previous positional exercises as it is an evolution from the tactical practices. The difference lies in the match-specificity of the contents. For instance, the purpose is to express the tactical principles under modelled competition situations. To be able to achieve this aim not many rules can be imposed, as the players will be over-constrained, thus limiting them.

A practical application of this type of practice is shown below:

Defensive Tactics in a 9 v 11 Numerical Disadvantage SSG

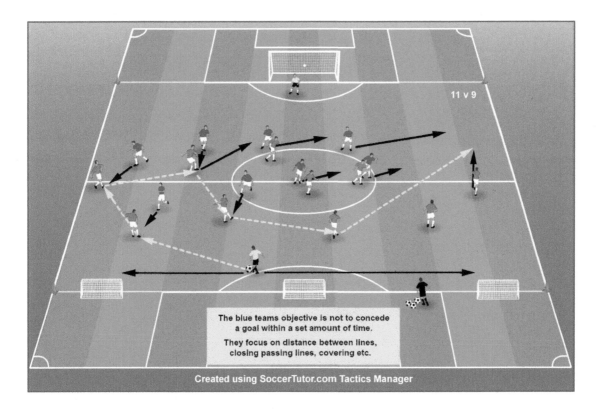

11 v 9

The blue teams objective is not to concede a goal within a set amount of time.

They focus on distance between lines, closing passing lines, covering etc.

Created using SoccerTutor.com Tactics Manager

Description

In the area between the 2 penalty areas, we play a 9v11 game and the blue team has a numerical disadvantage. Their aim is not to concede a goal within a set amount of time (coach's discretion). This organisation encourages the application of selected defensive tactical principles (distance between lines, closing passing lines, covering etc.) under a competitive game situation.

In addition to the principles that govern the tactical and competitive practices, the previous classification could be expanded by introducing other variables, such as the number of players involved, the organisation (blocks, lines, sectors), if the team is over or under loaded, the exact phases of play included etc.

However, the structure which has been presented aims to allow establishing practical methodological progressions, based on the principles and sub-principles that guide the playing model of the team. This perspective allows that, according to the standard of the players or the stage of the season, the practices can be focused on more basic (young players, first week of the season) or more complex (top-class players, competitive period) aspects.

As a summary, Table 1 (Page 46) shows the essential characteristics from each of the levels of complexity.

Periodization Fitness Training

2.3 HOW THE DYNAMIC OF THE EFFORTS ARE DISTRIBUTED

The second parameter used to classify the practices we use relies on how activities occur during the competition.

Player Analysis

Match analysis has been characterised by disclosing each of the performance dimensions of the players, isolating the conditioning, technical and tactical components, which has resulted in misleading interferences regarding the training process. The state-of-the-art research reveals that most of the papers published to date in the scientific literature have solely focused on determining the bioenergetics performance of the players.

Many computerised applications have been implemented during the last few years to quantify the volume and distribution of the conditioning demands experienced by footballers during match play. The primitive hand notation systems have been replaced by sophisticated procedures which allow us to determine the position of the players on the field in real time with image recognition programs (Mallo, 2006). The use of these systems, commercialised by companies such as Amisco or Prozone, have revealed that top-class players cover around 11 km during a game (Rampinini et al., 2004; Zubillaga, 2006; Bradley et al., 2007, 2009; Di Salvo et al., 2009). This parameter can be used as an overall estimation of the competition volume, but lacks importance if it is not accompanied by the intensity of the movements. The average distances covered at high speeds (speeds exceeding 14.4 km/h) and maximal intensities (speeds exceeding 19.8 km/h) by top-class players is 2.5 and 0.9 km per game respectively (Bradley et al., 2009), although the standard (Mohr et al., 2003) and type of competition (Dellal et al., 2011a), the playing position (Carling et al., 2008; Bradley et al., 2009; Di Salvo et al., 2009) and the team formation (Bangsbo, 2003) are factors that can affect these results.

In addition to these kinematical (the study of the motion of bodies without reference to mass or force) variables, the internal load which the competition represents has also been estimated after monitoring the heart rate response during matches. Due to the facility of its recording, it is an experimental technique widely employed to monitor the cardiovascular intensity of field activities (Achten & Jeukendrup, 2003). The average heart rate recorded during matches is approximately 85% of the individual maximal heart rate (HRmax) (Stolen et al., 2005).

Continuing with this line of research based on determining the conditional demands using certain devices under training environments, they can simultaneously record the external (by means of GPS) and internal (using heart rate monitors) workload has been extended.

Monitoring Player Sprints

At the same time as recording the total distance covered and high-speed activities, this technology allows us to estimate the number of accelerations (sprints) and decelerations carried out by the players. These highly demanding actions, which are associated to changes of speed or direction, have a great impact on muscles and joints, which increase the risk of incurring injuries. Recent studies have tried to more precisely report these movement requirements after calculating the metabolic power of each kind of activity (Osgnach et al., 2010; Colli et al., 2011).

The Misuse of Data

As accumulating match and training data has nowadays become so easy, in some situations this has led to losing perspective from the game itself. Some decades ago it was concluded that the majority of the goals occurred after short duration activities, with a low number of touches in the elaboration of the play and involving few players (Reep & Benjamin, 1968).

This statistic was wrongly interpreted by Scandinavian and Anglo-Saxons countries as; the more direct the attack is, the better chances to score a goal.

Data must be given a relative importance and should always be handled in a specific context analysis. Not respecting these considerations can derive to absurd situations, where people that have not seen the match or the training session are in charge of interpreting its meaningfulness from the data which has been recorded. As an example, some analysts might feel very proud for a player having a high number of minutes at an elevated cardiac intensity during a session.

Apparently, this could mean that the player has been actively involved in the play, but without seeing the actual situation. It could also be due to poor positioning, so this meant the player ran more and used up unnecessary energy, so this player may have in fact had a very inefficient game.

Adding Technical & Tactical Aspects to Player Analysis

It has not been until recent years when technical and tactical variables have started to be integrated into the scientific papers published in international literature (Lago & Martin, 2007; Lago, 2009; Tenga et al., 2010). These proposals enrich the object of study and allow a more qualitative interpretation of what happens during a match. It can be very important for a player to carry out a great number of high-intensity physical activities, but it is essential to know why he is doing them. A full back that reaches the opposition penalty box numerous times can have a great physical presence, but if his crosses are not precise, his performance will not have any significant effect on the collective benefit of the team. Using the same playing position as a reference, it will not be relevant if a player sprints a long distance to recover a defensive situation because of bad positioning.

The Eye of the Observer

The eye of the observer, even though it cannot be considered as a highly reliable tool from a scientific point of view, can provide extremely valid data for analysis purposes. Following the training sessions on a daily basis and exchanging relevant information with the players and all the other members of the staff can provide much more useful data than that of any out of context analysis. All the external sources have to be correctly managed to provide the correct feedback and improve the training system. They must always be treated as auxiliary complements and never as an end in themselves.

Intensity

The term intensity has been permanently associated to all the analysis carried out in modern football. In fact, it is strange for a manager not to list one of his characteristic features as being able to develop "intense" teams. Intensity has been habitually linked to the physical side, representing one of the traditional workload components (Platonov, 1988; Weineck, 1988; Verjoshanski, 1990).

The interpretation of this parameter should not be limited to the conditioning dimension, but should be seen as a wider conception that needs to be imposed throughout the levels of complexity defined in the previous section. Since the greatest number of training drills/practices in top class teams should be based upon the tactical and competitive levels, the playing intensity needs to be associated with the cognitive requirements to solve situations that the game raises. For instance, the traditional scheme of the tactical action developed by Mahlo (1969), composed of perceiving and analysing the situation, mentally solving the problem and executing a motor response, turns out to be especially relevant. Inherited from this thinking line, the concept of "intensity of concentration" (Mourinho, in Oliveira et al., 2007) appears as a determinant element to configure the dynamic of the effort in the training drills. The capacity to reach a selected attention towards the key tactical aspects is crucial in this sense.

Plenty of neuroscience features that would help to bring light to the importance of certain cognitive processes when playing football still remain unknown. For this reason, the great majority of fitness coaches move more easily stockpiling biometric parameters instead of investigating the issues that might influence

the learning process and the development of fatigue by the central nervous system. Thus, it can mean that the fitness coaches may think they have been successful and verify this in the post-match data sheet because their team has run further than the opposition, even though the team conceded a goal from a set piece situation in the last minute of the game. The team may have run large distances, but may have thus been too fatigued to maintain the necessary intensity of concentration until the end of the match.

The reverse situation could also occur with a team running less distance at a high-intensity in the course of a match due to having a better collective organisation. This could mean that they are running the optimum amount (due to good positioning) and are less fatigued. Again, it is necessary to carry out a global analysis which takes into account the realities of the game.

Mental Effects

The metabolic energy that a football match or training session represents has been estimated through indirect procedures. To do so, heart rate response has been monitored while the players are on the field and these values have been related to oxygen uptake measurements taken in laboratory settings. Despite this fact, one of the questions that remains uncertain is how to quantify the mental energy required to solve matchspecific problems.

What amount of mental energy does each training drill/practice require?

These cognitive requirements are not the same for each situation, as the presence or absence of the coach in a small sided game can have an effect on the intensity of concentration. In addition, there is not the same mental pressure when defending a corner kick in the last minute of a match with a 1-0 lead compared to when there is a 4-0 score. Furthermore, the cognitive demands are greater when taking a penalty in the World Cup final than during a friendly match.

The coach has to implement drills/practices that require the player to have the same intensity of thought as they do in competitive matches. To do

so, this book has established five theoretical levels of dynamics of efforts to classify the practices which should be employed during training as a habit. Table 2 (on the next page) on the next page shows these 5 levels which have been put into 3 main categories; low, medium and high intensity.

2.3.1 DYNAMIC OF THE EFFORTS; 5 LEVELS

Table 2: *Summary of Intensity Zones, Dynamic of Efforts and their Main Characteristics*

INTENSITY	DYNAMIC OF THE EFFORTS	DESCRIPTION
LOW	Low Intensive	Activities carried out far below the intensity of competition (active recovery - often used as warm downs).
MEDIUM	Medium Extensive	Activities carried out below the intensity of competition (non-regenerative).
HIGH	Long Intensive	Activities carried out at the same or above the intensity of competition and for a long duration.
	Short Intensive	Activities carried out above the intensity of competition, with short duration and incomplete recovery.
	Maximum Intensity	Maximum intensity activities; short duration and greater recovery.

LOW INTENSITY

The first of these dynamics is represented by the low intensity practices, which includes all the situations where the intensity of the effort is far below the requirements of a competitive match. This zone includes all the regenerative tasks oriented to achieve an active recovery which are used after a competitive match.

MEDIUM INTENSITY

The second kinds of practices are known as extensive efforts and are located in a, theoretical, medium intensity zone. Therefore, these activities include all the non-regenerative situations which are carried out below the intensity threshold of a competitive match.

At this stage, the following question could be raised:

Is it necessary to plan this kind of training drill/practice when the player needs a high intensity of concentration for the entire match (every minute)?

What Is the Right Level of Intensity?

It is not always the case that a fitness coach (or an assistant coach) has the opportunity to choose who to work with. Therefore, this will require him to have the capacity to adapt to different playing models and training styles. In some of these situations, the training direction might not be so clearly defined and many of the daily drills/practices could be included in this medium extensive effort section. It can be that the manager intentionally wants to work with this intensity, but sometimes, defects in the methods and organisation can lead to the practices not reaching an adequate intensity to stimulate the players. To confront these situations, the fitness/assistant coach

must develop an acute capacity to observe and detect inadequacies and design complementary drills to fulfil the training demands.

As previously indicated, coaches want their players to perform in a high intensity zone during the match. To achieve this the training sessions should be of a similar or higher intensity than competitive matches. The players need to be able to maintain an elevated performance for at least 90 minutes. However, if no tool can objectively measure the mental requirements of a task, how can the intensity of concentration be monitored?

This is one of the fundamental questions that limit the control of training workloads for many people. The way to channel the solution would be by developing a consequent training methodology. The session must have an indispensable budget which confines its environment (field availability, equipment, etc.) and, specially, with the players´ education to be able to train in a status of "tactical concentration" (Tamarit, 2007).

Even though seriousness and professionalism can characterise the great majority of elite teams training sessions, it is not so easy for footballers to achieve this mentality standard. For instance, Ricard (in Punset, 2011) recommends mental training to help to focus the attention and to learn how to concentrate. It is easy to recall past moments where one introduces himself so deeply in a task, with such a level of concentration, that energy flows naturally while even losing the concept of time. Voluntarily reaching this state of mental flow (Csikszentmihalyi, 1990) provides huge benefits and would be the final aim of the training methodology; facilitating the achievement of an absolute concentration in each practice by the player, to get the most from the session and to improve the capacities of the player and of the team.

Once an adequate working environment has been created and we have educated footballers towards a training philosophy, it can be further investigated which practices could help us achieve high intensity patterns.

Coaches should use the correct conditions (number of players, space, duration, constraints, etc.) to help the players adapt to the aims you want to achieve.

Recent studies suggest that the brain needs to be trained specifically for competition, as it has been demonstrated that mental fatigue impairs physical performance (Marcora et al., 2009). Interestingly, the brain behaves in a similar way as skeletal muscles do and, thus, its glycogen deposits are depleted after an exhausting exercise (Matsui et al., 2011) and a temporal adaptive response can occur inducing glycogen super-compensation (Matsui et al., 2012)

HIGH INTENSITY

Long Intensive & Short Intensive

Although conclusions based on scientific research are complicated for the footballer and coach, as the requirements of high standard competition are very different to the conditions of a laboratory set-up, the previous statements can help reinforce the idea that to be able to perform long duration intense exercise, the training should replicate this activity pattern. For the purpose of this book, these kinds of efforts have been called long intensive and are characterised by combining a high intensity with a long duration. According to the level of complexity (conditioning, technical, tactical or competitive) the practices will be structured in one or another way, as it will be explained in the next section.

In addition, Knicker (2011) reported that central fatigue can have a multi-factorial origin, which implies that the footballer has to not only be able to maintain a high level of mental intensity during the 90 minutes of a match, but also must find a solution for shorter periods of time when high and maximal intensity decisional demands are concentrated. The practices organised around short intensive efforts try to replicate this pattern of behaviour by grouping high demanding cognitive activities with an incomplete recovery between them.

These last two dynamics of efforts (long and short intensive) aim to decrease the effects that fatigue of the central nervous system might have on the footballers´ performance.

However, there are occasions where qualitative differences within players are not due to fatigue but to

Periodization Fitness Training

limiting performance factors. As an example, if a player confronts a 1v1 situation against the goalkeeper in the first minute of the game and makes a bad decision, it could be caused by a limiting factor (inability to decide correctly) rather than due to cognitive fatigue. If the same situation occurs in the last minute of the game, then fatigue could play a more relevant role in the picture.

Maximum Intensity

Maximum intensity training is structured towards the dynamic of efforts where, as a difference with the previous level, there is a greater recovery between the actions.

Speed and velocity have to be understood in modern football beyond a purely conditional perspective. They should be conceived as a global body comprising from the analysis of the situation to carrying out a motor response. The reduction of the space and time to think and act implies that those players who do not possess the capacity to perform maximum intensity efforts cannot survive in elite football. Therefore, speed acts as clearly differentiating criteria between performance standards.

Top-class players are able to resolve match specific problems with a higher velocity, anticipating what is going to happen as they have a better development of the perceptual, decision making and execution mechanisms. Several studies have addressed the perceptual and cognitive processes in football players and have concluded that those that compete at a higher standard are able to move the eyes faster to extract relevant information from the environment.

They analyse the posture of their opponents better to predict their actions and are able to identify familiar patterns which accelerates their responses (Ward et al., 2006; Vaeyens et al., 2007; North et al., 2009; Williams et al., 2011).

CONCLUSION

Even though the theoretical limits between these dynamics of efforts can be defined (Table 2), when stepping into practice the situation is not as easy.

The drills which do not contain the ball, or those arranged under technical activities, allow a more exact classification of the efforts. When a greater number of players are simultaneously involved the difficulty of the analysis increases as more variables are influencing the situation, such as individual capacities, teammates and opponents close or away from the ball, which team has more possession etc.

In any case, the coach has to design their training drills to include the majority of the footballers, while always respecting the individuality of each player's responses within it. In addition, the same drill/practice can have a different impact depending on the stage of the season. In general, the first time any practice is introduced it requires a greater cognitive demand on the players, as the control of the action relies on the conscious part of the brain. Once the practice is repeated, the control starts going to different areas of the brain (unconscious) with the subsequent energetic saving (Tamarit, 2007).

To take a practical example, the first time a coach practices an attacking pattern of play (11v0), the players require a high concentration level. If these routines are repeated every week and the movements become more mechanised, the activity control is moved to a different area of the brain cortex. This will be the case of a practice that goes from being high to medium intensity (of concentration). If the coach wants to increase the demands again, he can introduce different elements to alter the brain homeostasis (the brain resisting change) of the players; limit the number of ball touches, speed up play, add defenders etc.

60

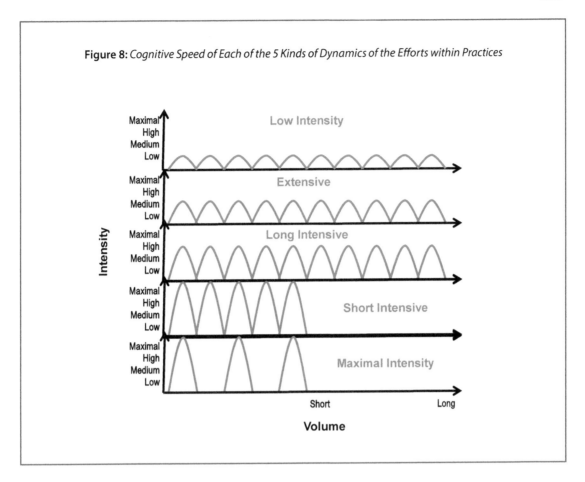

Figure 8: *Cognitive Speed of Each of the 5 Kinds of Dynamics of the Efforts within Practices*

Figure 8 intends to illustrate the relationship between intensity (of concentration) and volume for each of the five different kinds of practices outlined on the previous pages.

In a certain sense this represents the tempo (pace/speed) of the practice, showing the rhythm of the cognitive processes along its duration.

2.4 ORGANISATION OF THE TRAINING PRACTICES

This section provides an overview of a way to organise training drills/practices by converging the traditional views of managers and fitness coaches by combining the practices´ complexity (4 levels: conditioning, technical, tactical and competitive) with the dynamic of the efforts (5 types: low intensity, medium extensive, long intensive, short intensive and maximum intensity), as summarised in Figure 8.

This innovative approach aims to facilitate the design of methodological progressions and the workload periodization. The manager (or head coach) has to understand how by modifying the dynamic of the efforts he can use the same tactical drill/practice in different moments of the season. The fitness coach needs to be able to raise more complex training without losing their physiological objectives.

With this perspective the roles of the different coaches are not markedly differentiated as they request a common knowledge to design the tasks. At the end of the day, this should help to optimise training and increase the chances to obtain success in competition. Obviously, not all players will present the same response to the training, as the execution will be affected by their standard and also by the stage of the season the team is in. The principal aim of this section is to invite the reader to reflect on the topic and to be creative when planning their training sessions.

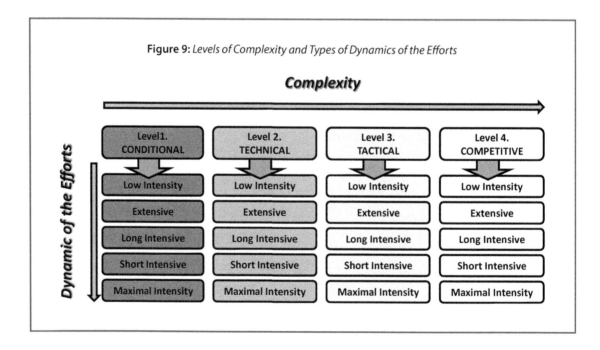

Figure 9: *Levels of Complexity and Types of Dynamics of the Efforts*

CONDITIONING PRACTICES

CONDITIONING PRACTICES

This level of complexity allows the greatest delimitation of workload components as it is founded on analytical and closed activities which are usually carried out on an individual basis, so sources of uncertainty are scarce as there is no interaction with teammates and opponents. This initial level represents the traditional approach to physical conditioning of footballers.

During many years, the players´ performance factors have been broken down into different components. Subsequently, these capacities have been treated in isolation, expecting a final functional improvement of the performance of the player due to the sum of these separated treatments.

The systemic conception of the human being blights this belief because the motor skills cannot be parcelled into strict compartments. For instance, this "divide and win" algorithm escapes from the permanent necessity that human beings have to be continuously organising themselves automatically and to be able to adapt to the environment (Pol, 2011). Hence, improving a conditional parameter, as it could be maximum oxygen intake by doing running sets, can influence a performance pre-requirement but for this gain to be effective it must be reorganised inside the motor control scheme of the player and adapted to a collective performance environment.

Low Intensity Conditioning

In the most basic stage, low intensity conditioning practices search for an active recovery effect on the players, without developing any physical capacity. As these tasks are carried out on the field the great majority of them will consist of steady-pace jogging or with slight changes of speed or in the form of displacement. In addition, on the field injury prevention exercises and warm downs could also be included under this category.

Low Intensity Interval Training   24 min

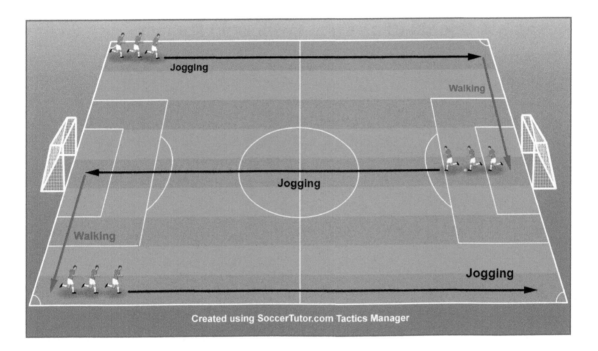

Created using SoccerTutor.com Tactics Manager

Description

The players alternate between jogging the length and walking half the width of the pitch as shown in the diagram.

Volume: 2 sets of 8 minutes with 4 minutes of stretching exercises after each set.

Medium Extensive Conditioning

Extensive conditioning practices are best characterised by an accumulation of efforts. In professional football, it seems unnecessary to use conditioning from this category due to the overall high training volume which players are already exposed to during a season. As match play demands are intermittent (constantly stopping and starting), it does not seem adequate to use steady pace running sets beyond the first re-adaptation stages after the off-season period or when coming back from an injury. This category would be formed by drills/practices oriented on improving aerobic capacity (running sets at a speed closed to the anaerobic threshold), strength-endurance or running technique drills. The evaluation of aerobic capacity should be done through tests that measure the individual anaerobic threshold.

Strength & Coordination Circuit with Light Running 24 min

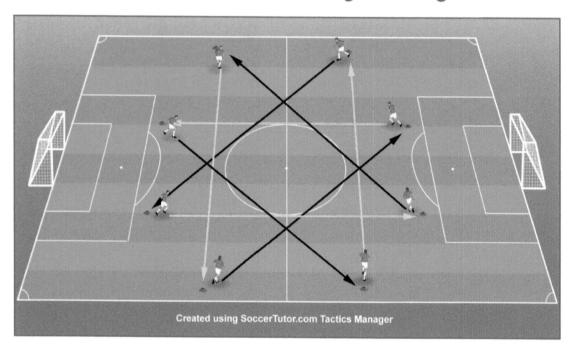

Created using SoccerTutor.com Tactics Manager

Description

A circuit is formed with 8 strength/coordination exercises performed on 8 different cones. The players do a 30 second exercise and then jog for 15 seconds to get to the next exercise.

Volume: 3 laps of 8 exercises (30 seconds work -> 15 seconds recovery) and 2 minutes of recovery between each lap.

Levels of Fatigue in the Latter Stages of Matches

During recent years several studies have reported that the physical performance of football players is impaired during the final stages of the match. Mohr et al. (2003, 2005) showed that distance covered at high-intensities decreased in the last 15 minutes in relation to the beginning of the match. Moreover, high intensity distances when their own team had possession of the ball were also effected in the later stages games (Bradley et al., 2009).

This decrease to the speed of physical efforts has been reinforced by the fact that players who came on as substitutes during a match produced 25% higher intensity and 63% more in terms of sprinting distance in the last 15 minutes of matches than those players who were not replaced (Mohr et al., 2003).

This conditional delivery reduction during the later stages of a match can have a multifactorial origin and glycogen depletion and dehydration could play an important role (Rahnama et al., 2003; Krustrup et al., 2004). However, it is very complicated to establish categorical conclusions regarding to which are the main causes of fatigue when the analysis only includes bio-energetic parameters. As previously indicated, fatigue of the central nervous system can be responsible for the greatest performance limitation.

Proceeding from this data, it would be interesting to examine if cognitive fatigue replicates a similar pattern to physical fatigue, by studying the evolution of perceptual, decision making and execution errors in the course of a match. There are plenty of psychological and volitional aspects that underlie match-day physical behaviour which need to be taken into account to have a global picture of the topic.

Long Intensive Conditioning

Long intensive conditioning practices aim to deal with this physical performance impairment in the later stages of a match. For instance, these practices search to improve the capacity of players to exercise at a high intensity during long periods and accelerating the recovery after intense periods (Bangsbo, 1994a). Therefore, the contents included in this category are generally the most classical fitness drills that football inherited from athletics; high speed running sets, interval training (fartlek) etc. Based on these exercises, other kinds of contents that replicate the intermittent displacements of players during matches can be designed. From a physiological point of view, the aim of these practices is to increase the amount of energy obtained within a unit of time with the priority on aerobic power and, therefore, maximum oxygen uptake is the parameter which has been traditionally employed to assess it.

Coordination & Agility Training in a Conditioning Circuit   24 min

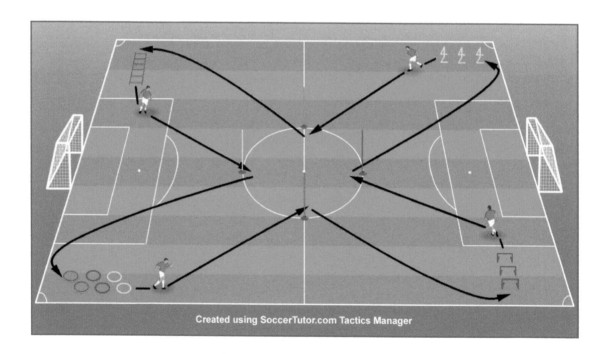

Created using SoccerTutor.com Tactics Manager

Description

This is a running circuit with 4 different coordinative exercises in each corner of the pitch. The players jog from the poles in the centre of the field to the corners. Once in the corner the players do the coordinative exercise (ladder, speed rings or hurdles), then run at a high intensity to the next pole in the centre of the field and to the next corner, until they complete a whole lap of the field. Each lap should take less than 4 minutes.

Volume: 4 laps (around 4 minutes each) and 2 minutes recovery between laps.

Levels of Fatigue after Short Intense Periods

Personal research (Mallo et al., 2007, 2009) carried out with football referees during the 2003 Under-17 World Cup and the 2005 Confederations Cup determined that, after the most intense 5 minute period of each half of the match, in the following 5 minutes the referees significantly decreased the amount of high-intensity activities performed.

Investigations with top-class footballers have also reported similar conclusions (Mohr et al., 2003; Bradley et al., 2009) so it could be hypothesised that there is an existence of a reversible and transitory physical fatigue after intense periods of the game. Classical Exercise Physiology studies (Balsom et al., 1992a,b; Dawson et al., 1993) have shown how intermittent physical performance can be affected by the duration, frequency and intensity of exercise and recovery phases.

When maximum intensity efforts are chained together without an adequate recovery between them, the sportsman's ability to carry out short duration intensive exercise is compromised. Disturbances in the ionic muscular homeostasis and alterations in the excitation of the sarcolemma (the membranous sheath of a muscle fiber) could, partially, help explain the temporary physical fatigue that might occur during a game (Bangsbo, 2004). The accumulation of potassium in the interstitium reduces muscle cells capacity to generate force (Cairris et al., 1995, in Bangsbo, 2003) and can induce this kind of fatigue (Bangsbo et al., 1996; Nordsborg et al., 2003; Mohr et al., 2005).

Short Intensive Conditioning

With the aim of limiting the incidence of the type of physical fatigue described on the previous page, short intensive conditioning practices attempt to stimulate the capacity to perform repeated intense efforts with the least impairment between them (Bangsbo, 1994b). On a practical level, these exercises are organised using consecutive maximum intensity sequences with an incomplete recovery between them, which has been known as developing repeated sprint (acceleration) ability (Fitzsimons et al., 1993).

The way the practices are organised can originate a different neuromuscular response, towards speed endurance or explosive strength endurance (see diagram below). The main difference in relation to the long intensive tasks lies in trying to increase the ability to produce energy faster as a priority for the lactic anaerobic pathway. It should always be respected that this capacity is always dependant on different aerobic variables (Meckel et al., 2009; Da Silva et al., 2010), as recovery between intense exercise is essential.

Coordination & Explosive Speed Endurance Circuit   24 min

PART A

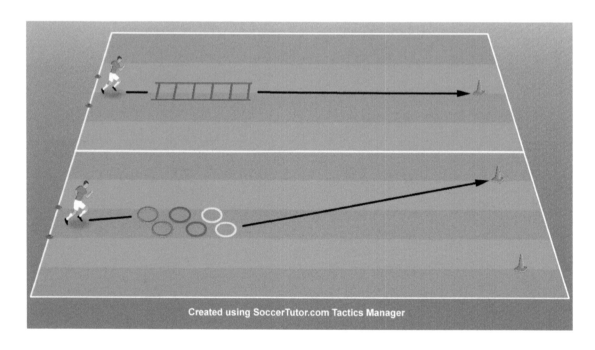

Created using SoccerTutor.com Tactics Manager

PART B

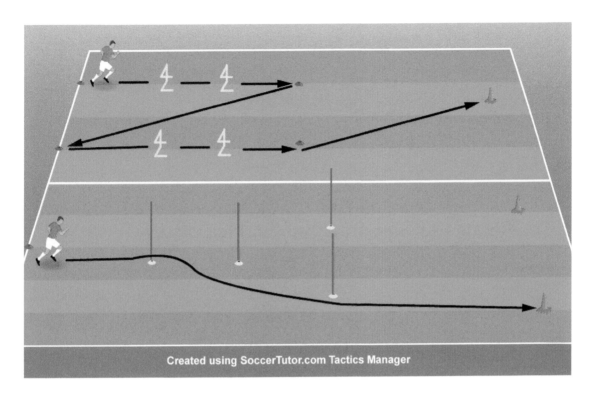

Created using SoccerTutor.com Tactics Manager

Objective

To develop conditioning for continuous short intensive and explosive movements/actions.

Description

The players complete 4 different explosive speed and coordination exercises within a continuous circuit.

The players start by performing a coordination exercise with the ladder (can use many variables for this) and then sprint 10 yards to the cone. They then jog slowly (recovery time) to the next position where they perform another coordination exercise with the speed rings, sprint 10 yards to a cone and jog slowly to the next position.

At the third station, the players jump over 2 small hurdles, change direction, jump over the next 2 hurdles and then sprint to the cone. They then jog slowly (recovery time) to the next position. Finally, the players run to the left or right of the first pole and then run round the furthest pole on the other side and sprint to the cone.

Volume: The players complete 3 full laps, with each including 1 minute of work and 1 minute recovery time. Include an extra 2 minutes of recovery time in between each lap.

Maximum Intensity Conditioning

Finally, maximum intensity conditioning practices are based on, as suggested by its name, short duration (less than 6 seconds) maximum intensity efforts with full recovery (at least 5 x working time) between them. The practices can be oriented to improve acceleration or explosive strength. The physiological purpose is to produce the highest amount of energy in the shortest time using the alactacid anaerobic pathway, through muscular adenosine-triphosphate (ATP) molecules and, in a second instance, re-synthesising ATP from Phosphocreatine. Performance in maximum intensity fitness tests, such as accelerating over short distances or jumping, has been linked to football players´ standard (Wisloff et al., 2004; Stolen et al., 2005). Nevertheless, it is complicated to say with certainty the percentage of this capacity genetically conditioned or that emerges as an adaptation to training.

Explosive Speed/Strength & Coordination Circuit   24 min

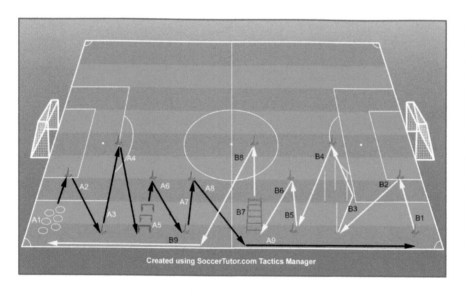

Created using SoccerTutor.com Tactics Manager

Description

We mark out the equipment and cones as shown in the diagram. The players complete this circuit which has 8 different components (+ 10 recovery walks). Split the players into 2 groups and they start from A1 and B1 respectively.

The players perform a maximum intensity activity (5 seconds) which is always from the cone closest to the touchline (A1, A3, A5, A7, B1, B3, B5 and B7).

They then walk (recovery time of 30 seconds) to the next cone. These recovery walks are at A2, A4, A6, A8, B2, B4, B6 and B8).

After completing the circuit in one half of the field, the players walk half the length of the field to extend the recovery (A9 and B9), and start again from the opposite corner (B1 or A2).

Volume: 3 full laps (A1-A9 and B1-B9). Add an extra 2/3 minutes recovery time between laps.

Periodization Fitness Training

TECHNICAL PRACTICES

Low Intensity Technical Practices

The second of the levels of complexity is directed towards football specific coordinative skills, where the use of the ball is necessary.

Low intensity technical practices have the aim of securing an active recovery of the player and can be included the day after a match or following a demanding training period.

Pairs 4 Zone Football Tennis Game   24 min

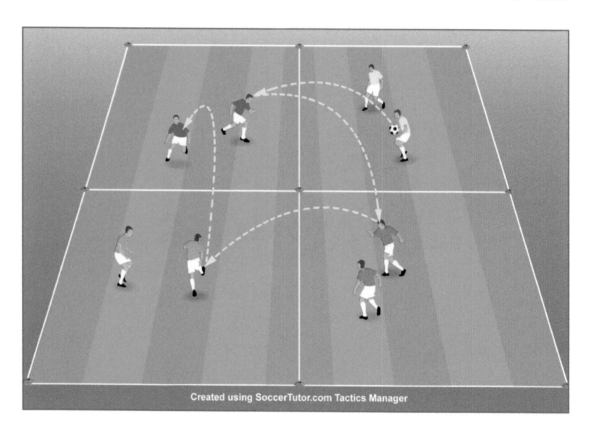

Created using SoccerTutor.com Tactics Manager

Description

In an area 10 x 10 yards, the players are divided into pairs with each pair in one zone. The teams can attack any of the other 3 squares.

Adapt the rules to the age/level of the players e.g. 1 touch, 2 touches, allow 1 bounce etc.

Volume: 2 sets of 10 minutes (changing the rules for second set) and 2 minutes recovery after each set.

Periodization Fitness Training

Medium Extensive Technical Practices

The next step is formed by extensive technical practices, which are frequently employed during training. The execution demands higher requirements on the footballers than the warm ups with the ball. To achieve an adequate pace, the players need to be fully concentrated throughout. The technical work is more detailed and specific; small groups, passing routines, shooting with goals, crossing and finishing, etc.

Passing Combination Play with Crossing & Finishing   *24 min*

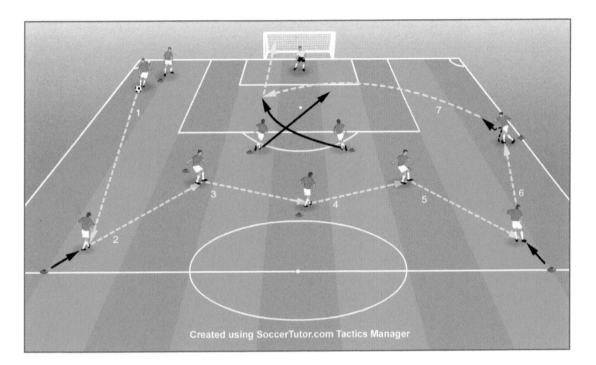

Created using SoccerTutor.com Tactics Manager

Description

A minimum 10 players (+GK) take part in this circuit and the players have to move through all positions to complete a lap. The passes are in the order shown in the diagram.

At the first 6 positions, after playing the ball, the player then runs to the next position. The 7th player takes a touch towards the byline and crosses for the 2 players in the middle. One player moves to the start position and 7 moves into the middle to try and score next time.

Volume: 4 sets (5 minutes each) with 1 minute recovery in between each set. In each set the direction and the kind of passing sequence should be modified.

Long Intensive Technical Practices

Long intensive technical practices imply exercising at a high-intensity for a long duration. Proceeding from a technical drill, to fulfil this objective, space and acting times need to be adapted. One of the major applications of this kind of structures is during the re-adaptation of a footballer after an injury, as it allows developing specific motor skills under controlled situations, at the same time of achieving a high physiological response.

Studies carried out with Norwegian footballers have shown that technical circuits, based on dribbling the ball in different trajectories (Hoff et al., 2002; Stolen et al., 2005) produced an important cardiovascular stimulus (average heart rate; 92-94% of HRmax). In these circuits players worked for 4 blocks of 4 minutes with a 3 minute active recovery period between each block. This work rate profile seems to be effective to achieve the physiological objectives and it appears interesting to include a greater variety of skills in the practices.

Technical Dribbling Circuit Training   24 min

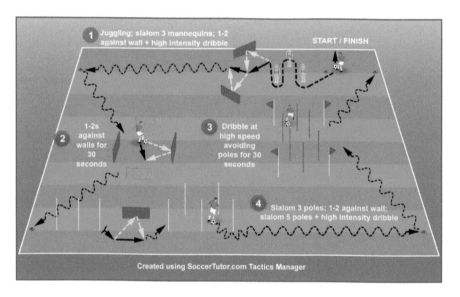

Description

This is a technical circuit with 4 kinds of exercises done at full intensity. When dribbling between the 4 exercises this is recovery time so should be at a slow pace.

1. We use a full sized pitch and start in the upper right corner. The players juggle the ball, dribble through the mannequins, play 1-2 combinations against both walls and finish with a high intensity dribble to the end of the field.
2. Players perform 1-2 combinations with as many walls as possible within 30 seconds.
3. The players dribble through the poles, play a 1-2 touch against the wall, slalom through 5 poles with changes of direction and finish with high intensity dribble to the end of the field.
4. Different dribbling sequences between the poles for 30 seconds.

Volume: 4 laps (4 minutes per lap) and 2 minutes recovery time after each.

Short Intensive Technical Practices

In the case of short intensive technical practices, maximum intensity working periods have to be organised, with an incomplete recovery between them. Different skills are grouped together in a small space which can be used to achieve this aim.

Passing and Movement in an Acceleration Hexagon   24 min

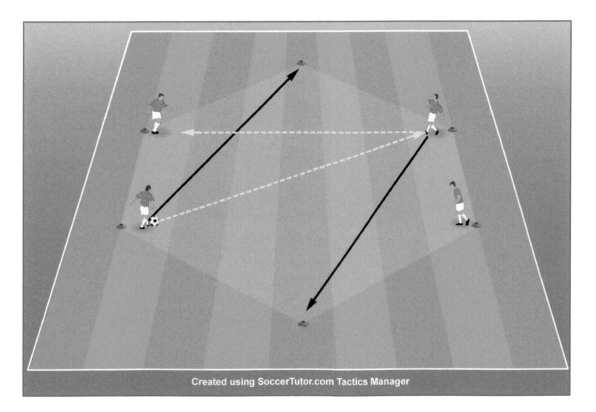

Created using SoccerTutor.com Tactics Manager

Description

4 players are in a hexagon with 10 yard sides and perform 12 sets. Different technical sequences can be used in each set. The example shown in the diagram is that a player controls the ball, passes to any teammate and accelerates to an empty cone.

Change the sequence for every set. Other variations are control, play 1-2 touch with an outside player and accelerate to an empty cone; the same and play to a third man; dribble and change direction in the middle; pass and press the teammate, etc.

Volume: Players perform 12 sets of 1 minute with 1 minute recovery in between each set.

Maximum Intensity Technical Practices

Each pair should have 5-6 repetitions per set and each repetition should take around 5 seconds, with 45 seconds recovery time between each repetition. Unlike the previous page, maximum intensity technical practices require a complete recovery between the repetitions. For instance, 5-6 seconds of maximum intensity technical skills requires 30-45 seconds of recovery time so pauses between them can be planned.

Timing Forward Runs, Combination Play & Finishing   24 min

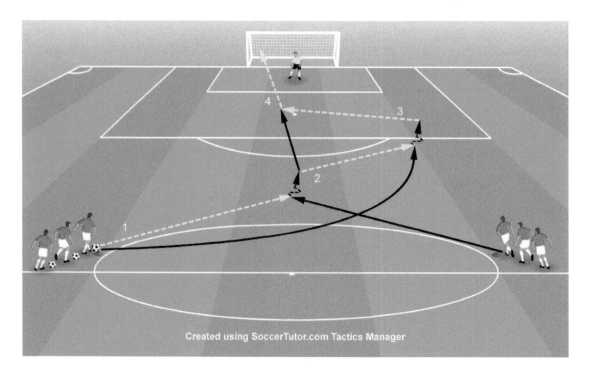

Description

The players work in pairs, one on each cone near the halfway line. The first player passes to their partner and then makes an overlapping run. The second player passes the ball into the space for the first player to run onto. That player then chooses whether to shoot from outside the box or pass into the box for the second player to finish (as shown in diagram).

The passing sequences and the way to finish can be changed in each set.

Volume: Perform 4 sets (5 minutes each) with 1 minute recovery time in between each set.

Each pair should have 5-6 repetitions per set and each repetition should take around 5 seconds, with 45 seconds recovery time between each repetition.

TACTICAL PRACTICES

TACTICAL PRACTICES

From this level of point onwards the dynamic of the efforts control is not as evident, as the presence of teammates and opponents means there is more unpredictable behaviour in the play. In any case, the practices are based upon the selection of certain principles and subprinciples which are developed under a preferential activity pattern. Again, it needs to be stressed that the intensity of the decision process is what puts the effort into context (Frade, in Díaz, 2012).

The uncertain and changing nature that football represents implicates that exercise and recovery periods do not always have the same rhythm, so the repetitive method (Solé, 2006) results in a very interesting proposal for team sports. Varying the practices, rest periods, using sets and repetitions within a practice gives the players a changing stimulus to satisfy their adaptation potential.

Low Intensity Tactical Practices

Low intensity tactical practices are not very often included in the day-to-day schedule of topclass teams. Tactical work always implies a cognitive component so, if the aim is to facilitate the recovery of the player, tactical drills could go in the opposite direction generating a greater (mental) fatigue. These kinds of contents are more commonly introduced in the beginning of the session or in a morning session on a match-day. The diagram presents an example of a positional practice used to explain the team positioning and organisation when the opposition has the ball. The execution can be very similar to tactical warm ups shown in section 2.1.2 and can serve as a basis to progress into more complex contents.

Tactical Shape & Collective Movements in Relation to the Position of the Ball
24 min

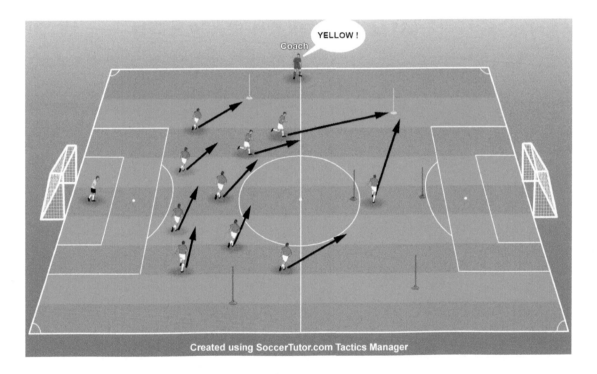

Created using SoccerTutor.com Tactics Manager

Description

The players take their defensive positions inside the playing formation of the team. Different colour poles are located around the field. The coach calls out a colour and the players have to adopt the team defensive position in relation to where that pole (ball) is.

Volume: The players perform 2 sets of 8 minutes with 2 minutes recovery after each set.

Medium Extensive Tactical Practices

Extensive tactical practices are based on the highest possible concentration requirements. As previously indicated, the classification is closely related to the grade of brain control requested to solve the situation. For instance, this category includes the most repeated and mechanised tactical activities, with a lower necessity of control by the conscious part of the brain. A position specific zonal game (as shown below) can be used to illustrate these types of practices.

The first time this content is used in training may require an elevated intensity of concentration from the players, so they are able to play the ball with precision while respecting the rules. Once this is repeated on various occasions, the players adopt a more automatic behaviour which reduces the demands placed on the motor cortex of the brain.

Position Specific 8 (+2) v 3 Zonal Possession Game   18 min

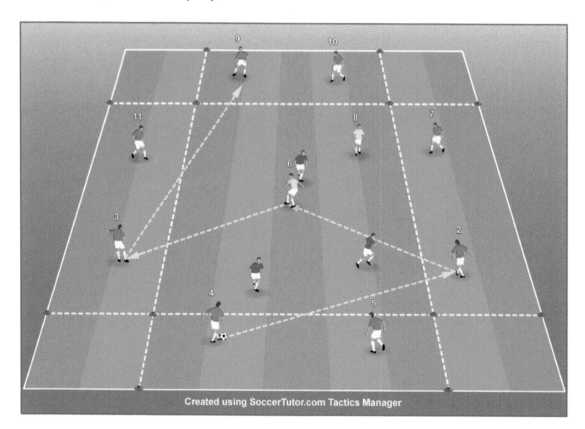

Created using SoccerTutor.com Tactics Manager

Periodization Fitness Training

Description

In a 15 x 15 yard square, we work with 13 players (you can adapt this depending on the number of players in your training session). 8 players are positioned in the 4 zones outside the central square, while 2 floating players (yellow) and 3 defenders (blue) play inside.

The 8 players outside the main square are in their specific positional role. We have 2 centre backs in 1 outside zone and 2 forwards in the one opposite. We also have the left back and left midfielder in the zone on the left, with the right back and right midfielder in the zone on the right. 2 centre midfielders (yellow) act as floater players inside the main square.

Volume: 3 sets of 5 minutes with 1 minute recovery time after each set.

The rules can be modified in each set; 2 touches outside/1 touch inside; 1 touch outside/2 touches inside; everyone is limited to 1 touch, etc.

Coaching Points

High-demanding practices which require an intensity of concentration feed the training process and, therefore, require a precise methodological organisation.

The coach has to manage components such as the number of players involved (teammates and opponents), space, time and rules or constraints, to achieve the tactical conducts in the expected and required form.

Long Intensive Tactical Practices

Long intensive tactical tasks are organised with a greater number of players than short intensive ones, which enriches tactical interactions (see diagram below). Playing space has to be big to permit a low density (number of players per playing surface) and the duration of each set has to be long enough to favour the occurrence of the wanted performances. This way of organising the drills has a varied nomenclature in the literature despite the fact that, for almost all the authors, presents similar features. Thus, Jose Mourinho (in Oliveira et al., 2007) calls them "dynamic specific", as they allow experiencing the greater principles of the playing model, representing a more real situation. At the same time, Sanz (2010), who is one of the coaches that more investigated these training drills more, terms them as "big spaces", whereas Pol (2011) denominates them "extensive" and they are included in the training sessions with a sub-dynamic oriented to "duration" (Tamarit, 2007).

Possession Play and Fast Break Attacks in an 11 v 11 Dynamic Central Zone Game

30 min

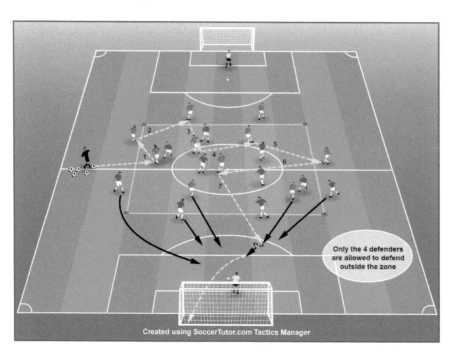

Only the 4 defenders are allowed to defend outside the zone

Created using SoccerTutor.com Tactics Manager

Description

We mark out a zone in the centre as shown in the diagram. Each team has 6 players inside who aim to keep possession with the support of their 4 defenders who are positioned outside as shown.

Once a team completes a pre-determined number of consecutive passes, they can play outside the square trying to score in the big goal and only the opposition's 4 defenders outside the square can defend the situation.

Volume: Perform 3 sets of 8 minutes with 2 minutes recovery after each set.

The Impact of Space and Time

Although the main target of the practices in this section is to generate pre-fixed tactical behaviours, it is interesting to know how playing spaces and time can impact the physiological response of players. Personal studies (Mallo & Navarro, 2008) have suggested that a minimum of 100 m2 per player involved in the practice are needed to be able to reach an adequate conditional stimulus (distance covered at a high intensity, time employed exercising above 85% HRmax, etc.). From a practical point of view, if a ball possession exercise involving 16 players (7v7 plus 2 neutral players) wants to be implemented following this regimen of effort, the space should be around 1600 m2 (for example, 40 x 40 yard square or 50 x 32 yard rectangle). This density pattern is an estimation and not a standard law as, in reality, density should increase exponentially and not linearly to the number of players taking part in the task.

Regarding the duration of practices, it has been documented that it takes two or three minutes for a sportsman to reach their maximum oxygen uptake running on a treadmill (Hoff, 2005). However, football players do not perform straight line running at constant speeds during a game, as they are moving intermittently with an alternative participation in the play, which means they need more time to achieve an important cardiovascular stimulus. Thus, taking as a reference the research carried out by Bansgbo (1994c) and Helgerud et al. (2001), it could be hypothesised that a minimum of 4 minutes high intensity periods would be needed to stimulate the maximum oxygen uptake during these kinds of practices.

This set length of the practice aims to guarantee that all players are actively involved in the play and should be proportional to the number of players involved. Based on practical experiences, it could be recommended that each working set should have a duration equivalent to multiplying the number of players involved by 30 seconds. Using the previous example, if 16 players take part in a possession game, each set should be around 8 minutes long.

The recovery time between sets should be no longer than 2-3 minutes to achieve an accumulative effect, and should be used for pertinent tactical corrections, introducing variations or hydrating. These space and time references are only an indication, as each training environment needs individual adjustments.

Short Intensive Tactical Practices

Short intensive tactical practices should involve a low number of players to achieve the right cognitive intensity (as shown in the diagram on the next page). The remaining configuration parameters have to also be manipulated. Therefore, if the playing surface is reduced, the players are forced to think faster as they have less time to perceive, decide and execute.

The duration of the sets has to be shorter as it is impossible to maintain maximum mental intensity over long periods. The rules of the practices can be modified to obtain a higher concentration of the desired tactical activities; pressing after losing the ball, always creating 2v1 attacking situations, man-to-man marking, etc.

This organisation allows the players to experience the sub-principles of the sub-principles, which have a lower complexity as they represent a further division of the playing model (Mourinho, in Oliveira et al., 2007). This author calls this activity pattern "elevated specific tension regimen", whereas Sanz (2010) categorises them as "reduced spaces" and Pol (2011) as "intensive (action)".

During recent years, many studies (Owen et al., 2004, 2011; Little & Williams, 2007; Kelly & Drust, 2009; Hill-Haas et al., 2010, 2011; Dellal et al., 2011b,c, 2012a,b) have addressed the effect that the modification of the components and constraints (frequency and duration of sets, number of teammates, opponents and neutral players, number of touches, etc.) of short intensive tactical practices have in the physical and technical workload. These studies can provide coaches with valuable information when incorporating these practices into their training sessions/program.

Short Intensive Tactical 4 v 4 Possession Game   16 min

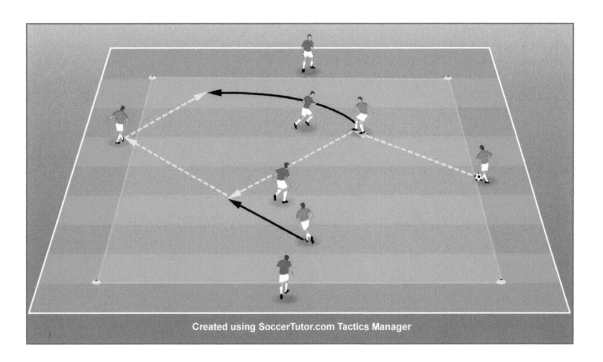

Created using SoccerTutor.com Tactics Manager

Objective

To work on short intensive conditioning with possession play; passing and player movement.

Description

In a 15 x 15 yard area, 2 teams of 4 players compete in a possession game. Inside the square, there is a 2v2 situation and 2 players from each team provide support from outside of the square in the positions shown.

Volume: Perform 2 full sets which include 3 repetitions of 1 minute work (inside the square) and 1 minute active recovery (outside the square). Also add 2 minutes full recovery time after each set.

The rules are changed in every repetition e.g. Limit the inside players to 2 touches and the outside players to 1 touch; limit all players to 1 touch, etc.

Maximum Intensity Tactical Practices

Finally, maximum intensity tactical practices require quality execution of these types of short duration activities with a complete recovery in between them. The simplest organisation results from including few players in the activity, as the diagram below shows, and from there on the complexity of the practices can be increased. The presence of the ball and opponents lengthens the work periods in relation to the maximum intensity conditional tasks, to allow the tactical activities to occur.

This kind of practice has been called "elevated velocity contraction" by Jose Mourinho (in Oliveira et al., 2007) and the tactical concerns are focused towards the sub-principles. Pol (2011) uses the concept of "intensive dynamic (interaction)" to group the practices which request short-duration quick responses on the players, which need to be integrated with those of the teammates.

Maximum Intensity 8 v 2 Attacking Combination Play   20 min

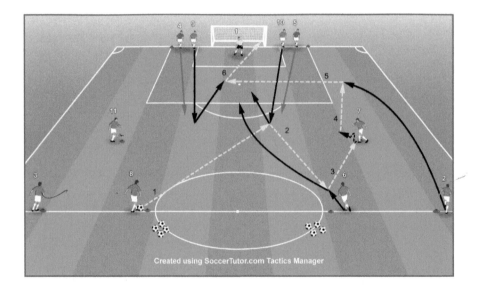

Description

The players work on attacking combinations against 2 defenders. The centre backs and forwards start from the end line as shown in the diagram.

The forward provides support to the centre midfielders and from then on, any kind of attacking play can be built. The players just have to make sure to always finish the attack with maximum intensity. The coach can change the kind of attacking combinations.

Volume: Perform 2 sets of 8 minutes with 2 minutes recovery after each set. Each attacking play should be a maximum of 10 seconds and the players have 50 seconds recovery before starting the next one.

COMPETITIVE
SMALL SIDED GAMES

Low Intensity Competitive Practices

This fourth level of complexity is represented by competitive situations, where constraints are limited to ensure a greater similarity with real match play. The concept of low intensity competitive practices carries a great inconsistency as the terms competition and low intensity seem to be conflictive. For instance, should any practice be implemented in this category, the recreational component would be the focus (example shown below).

Creating Space and Passing in a 9 v 9 Small Sided Game   18 min

Description

Two teams play a normal small sided game in a small space (9v9). If every player manages to touch the ball without the opposition touching the ball before a goal is scored, the goal counts double.

Volume: 2 sets of 6 minutes with 3 minutes of stretching exercises after each set.

Medium Extensive Competitive Practices

Extensive competitive practices involve all the forms where the decisional intensity is below the competition threshold (see diagram example below). This category could be built with practices with this aim, as a non-constrained game in the final part of a training session so players have fun after a high intensity and demanding session. Alternatively, these can be used with practices that do not reach the expected requirements due to organisation problems, as it can happen when too many players take part in a small space.

Half a Pitch 9 v 9 (+2) Small Sided Game   24 min

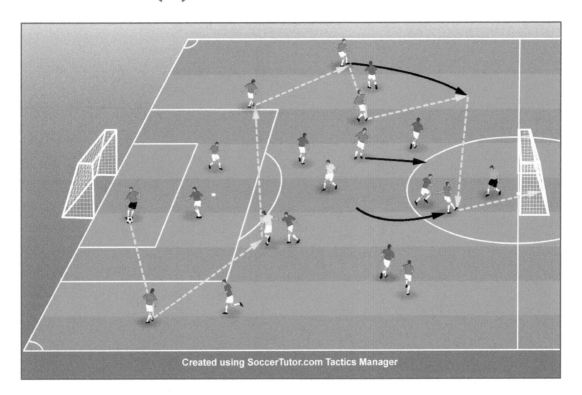

Created using SoccerTutor.com Tactics Manager

Description

We play a normal 9v9 game using half a full sized pitch, with 2 neutral players who play with the team in possession.

Volume: 2 sets of 10 minutes with 2 minutes recovery after each set.

Long Intensive Competitive Practices

Long intensive competitive practices represent the highest level of specificity in relation to match play (example below). Thus, the considerations shown in the previous pages (greater number of players, big space and long duration) must be respected to reach high mental focus. As goalkeepers take part in the practices and the offside law is applied, this affects the amount of "useful" available space. The space per number of players involved must be above the 100 m2 relationship explained in the previous section.

Match Specific 8 v 8 SSG with Offside Rule   30 min

Created using SoccerTutor.com Tactics Manager

Description

In an area 70 x 40 yards we play an 8v8 small sided game. Both teams are in a 3-3-1 formation with 3 defenders, 3 midfielders and 1 forward. The offside rule is applied throughout so the players have to manage the space (more limited) as they have to in competitive matches.

Volume: 3 sets of 8 minutes with 2 minutes recovery time after each set.

Short Intensive Competitive Practices

Short intensive competitive practices are made different from the previous ones by the presence of a lower number of players who play in a smaller space and for shorter periods of time (example practice below). These types of practices require a higher number of eccentric contractions (a type of muscle contraction that occurs as the muscle fibres lengthen) such as accelerating, decelerating, changes of direction etc, so their use has to be cautiously selected during the training sessions.

Short Intensive 4 v 4 Small Sided Games   24 min

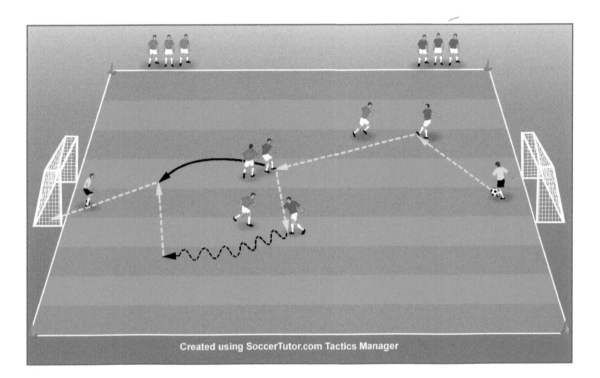

Created using SoccerTutor.com Tactics Manager

Description

Two teams of 7 players (1 goalkeeper + 6 outfield players) are in an area 30 x 20 yards. 3 outfield players from each team play a short intensive game while the other 3 players are recovering outside.

Volume: Each group of 3 players performs 6 sets of 2 minute 3v3 (+ goalkeepers) games with 2 minutes recovery time after each set (while the other 3 teammates play).

Maximum Intensity Competitive Practices

The last of the categories is represented by maximum intensity competitive practices. The number of players taking part in these practices influences the working periods, as the greater number of participants, the larger the duration to enable the coach to monitor the quality and issue instructions. An alternative to organise these practices can be to implement short games in a space with a high density of players, allowing a long recovery between them. As the diagram below shows, practices including an alternative participation of 3 or 4 teams can help achieve this dynamic of efforts.

Maximum Intensity SSG with Outside Support Players   15 min

Description

Two teams of 8 outfield players plus 2 goalkeepers play in a 30 x 30 yard square. Each team has 4 outfield players on the inside and an extra 4 players (in the positions shown) who provide support outside the square in the attacking half. The aim is to play with maximum intensity, trying to score quickly with help from the outside players.

Volume: Perform 10 sets of 90 seconds (swap the inside and outside players every 90 seconds).

2.5 THE FINAL PART OF THE SESSION

This is probably the part of the session which, traditionally, has been given the least amount of attention and importance. Without trying to generalise too much, most of the times it is limited to stretching exercises while physiological parameters return to base values.

This can be a good moment to carry out a brief evaluation of the session, trying to provide the players with short and precise information, to reinforce the work they have done.

With professional football players this final part should be linked with individualised development programs (tactical analysis, mental training, gym, etc.). From here on, as the aim is for players to arrive at the next training session in the best condition possible, physiotherapy, hydration and nutrition play a vital role to fulfil this objective.

CHAPTER 3

PERIODIZATION

PERIODIZATION

It is appropriate to define some terms which are habitually employed when this topic is addressed before going deeper into the essence of this chapter. According to Sánchez Bañuelos (1997) the concept of planning implies a global perspective of the teaching and learning process, where the intentions are declared and the capacity to decide about all relevant aspects of the training organisation exists. Another extended word is programming, which reflects a more practical approach to the object of study representing the way to achieve in the session, by selecting adequate contents for the aims set out when planning. Due to the conceptual scope of both terms, this chapter is focused on periodization, which is understood as the organisation of the season into smaller periods and units (Issurin, 2008).

Therefore, and from all of the above, periodization helps a coach to select the best moments to introduce certain types of training practices. That is, once the coach has all his pieces (training practices), periodization would help him to build the puzzle.

The classic textbooks of Theory and Practice of Training show plenty examples of periodization models. However, the great majority of these models have been taken from individual sports and you should not simply use the same methods as team sports are very different. Fundamental factors to examine are how it will disrupt the performance level of the team, which would be influenced by the possibilities of the players to carry out training sessions. In a very general way, three levels have been identified in this book to classify the training availability of the teams.

Elite Professional Teams

The highest level would be represented by professional teams which take part in more than one competitive match per week. Hence, this level could be represented by all elite European clubs which participate in international competitions (Champions League, Europa League, etc.). These teams are characterised by presenting an elevated competitive density which forbids going beyond the succession of pre-match warm ups, match-day and post-match recovery sessions. The case of the Spanish team Athletic de Bilbao during the 2011-2012 season could illustrate this level of performance. As this team took part in the national league ("La Liga") and had success in both the national ("Copa del Rey") and international (Europa League) cups, the eam was involved in a total of 63 competitive matches during the season. When travel and other delays (flights, delays in airports, coach trips, hotel stays, etc.) are added, the mental and physical burden which players are subjected to in this standard of teams is considerable. The amount of training therefore must be much lower than in other teams.

Professional Teams

The second level is formed by those professional teams who generally play one match per week. The managers of these teams have absolute freedom to design the training schedule, so this is the level which allows greater and richer periodization possibilities. During most parts of the season the interval between matches ranges between 6 and 8 days and can be influenced by external factors such as the broadcaster's television selections.

Semi Professional & Amateur Teams

The last level would include all the teams where the footballers are unable to have an exclusive dedication for the sport, so training times are more limited. These teams usually train late in the afternoon or evening, with the players arriving to the training ground once they have finished their working or studying day. In some cases, the available training time (usually four sessions per week) should not be a limiting factor, although it is crucial to control the demands which

the players are subjected to. The players should not be exposed to excessive fatigue as they present a greater difficulty to carry out posteffort recovery processes.

The Training Load

Some fundamental training principles need to be considered for all different types of teams. The General Adaptation Syndrome (Seyle, 1950) explains how, when an external stimulus is applied to the body, there is an alteration of its homeostasis. If this stimulus is maintained over time, the body adapts and tries to develop a resistance to confront a similar kind of stress which could appear in the future. If the stimulus is too intense, the body enters an exhaustion phase where catabolic processes are predominant. Training adaptation replicates the same phenomenon where the task workload, the fatigue that is generated and the necessary recovery to assimilate it are the key parameters to be managed by the coaches.

The training load represents the stimulus offered to the football player which must exceed the individual threshold in order to achieve beneficial effects (Navarro, 2001). This aspect should not be limited to the physical plane, as it should also imply the cognitive dimension. Subjecting the body to constant intensity stimulus will limit or stop their effectiveness, as an adjustment will occur in which all the information that has not reached the excitability threshold of the receptors will not be effective. The solution does not consist in going to the opposite extreme, as changing the drills continuously can lead to a sensorial over-excitation and an impaired capacity to absorb information. Altogether, this requires a continuous adjustment of the stimulus in accordance to the standard of the players which they are directed to.

Tactical fatigue is generated as a consequence of applying a load that exceeds the individual effort threshold. Each kind of applied workload requires a different recovery time for its assimilation and to improve the performance level above his initial values, a phenomenon known as super-compensation.

The Challenge for a Coach

The great challenge for coaches is to organise training in such a way that the players can experience (tactical) super compensations from programming the practices in the different cycles during a season.

This adequate workload dosage and sequencing would enable a summation of positive effects. On the other hand, if the loads are condensed in a short period of time, the footballer can be induced to an excessive fatigue, as the assimilation processes which guarantee a correct recovery cannot be completed. In addition, when the loads are far away from each other there are no benefits as the structural changes needed for progression are not achieved.

Training periodization tries to solve the problem of organising the loads, in order to achieve the highest team performance during a season. This season can be divided into smaller temporal units using a varied nomenclature (periods, phases, cycles, blocks, etc.) depending on the planning model used as a reference (Navarro, 2001). With a short-term perspective, the loads can be periodized in the interval of time between two competitive matches.

The terms macro-structure and micro-structure used in the next sections have been adapted after studies carried out by Seirul·lo (1987, 2003), Solé (2006) and Roca (2011). The temporal distribution of the workloads in those structural levels will be examined in depth during the ollowing pages, always respecting the specificity of football training.

3.1 MACRO-STRUCTURE OF PERIODIZATION

Traditional models based on individual sports (Matveiev, 1981; Harre, 1982; Bompa, 1999) started the season with a very long preparation period, composed of a generic and a specific phase, looking to achieve the fitness peak at the right moment of the season during the competitive period.

The physical capacities were simultaneously developed during the preparation period, trying to obtain a super-compensation of all the previous work coinciding with the principal competition of the calendar. These models were translated to football, with players being subjected to a high volume of conditioning exercises during the preparation period. This was followed by a more specific type of work during the competitive period.

During the last years, the length of the period has been extended. This has meant that football players have had to increase their competitive frequency, as they need to perform at their peak in different stages of the season.

Taking up the previous example from Athletic de Bilbao in the 2011-2012 season, Figure 10 shows the competition density of this team. This case can serve to question the application of traditional periodization models in football, as it seems very complicated to claim that a 5-6 week preparation period, typically known as preseason, would be sufficient to guarantee an optimal performance during a 9-10 months long competition period (Carli et al., 1982; Baker et al., 1994; Schneider et al., 1998; Baker, 2001; Gamble, 2006; Newton et al., 2006).

Figure 10: *Competition Calendar of Athletic de Bilbao during the 2011-2012 Season*

	M	T	W	T	F	S	S	M	T	W	T	F	S	S	M	T	W	T	F	S	S	M	T	W	T	F	S	S	M	T	W	T	F	S	S	M	T
JULY															11	12	13	14	15	16	17	18	19	20	21	22	23	24	25	26	27	28	29	30	31		
AUGUST	1	2	3	4	5	6	7	8	9	10	11	12	13	14	15	16	17	18	19	20	21	22	23	24	25	26	27	28	29	30	31						
SEPTEMBER				1	2	3	4	5	6	7	8	9	10	11	12	13	14	15	16	17	18	19	20	21	22	23	24	25	26	27	28	29	30				
OCTOBER						1	2	3	4	5	6	7	8	9	10	11	12	13	14	15	16	17	18	19	20	21	22	23	24	25	26	27	28	29	30	31	
NOVEMBER		1	2	3	4	5	6	7	8	9	10	11	12	13	14	15	16	17	18	19	20	21	22	23	24	25	26	27	28	29	30						
DECEMBER				1	2	3	4	5	6	7	8	9	10	11	12	13	14	15	16	17	18	19	20	21	22	23	24	25	26	27	28	29	30	31			
JANUARY							1	2	3	4	5	6	7	8	9	10	11	12	13	14	15	16	17	18	19	20	21	22	23	24	25	26	27	28	29	30	31
FEBRUARY			1	2	3	4	5	6	7	8	9	10	11	12	13	14	15	16	17	18	19	20	21	22	23	24	25	26	27	28	29						
MARCH				1	2	3	4	5	6	7	8	9	10	11	12	13	14	15	16	17	18	19	20	21	22	23	24	25	26	27	28	29	30	31			
APRIL							1	2	3	4	5	6	7	8	9	10	11	12	13	14	15	16	17	18	19	20	21	22	23	24	25	26	27	28	29	30	
MAY		1	2	3	4	5	6	7	8	9	10	11	12	13	14	15	16	17	18	19	20	21	22	23	24	25											

Light Grey: National league (La Liga) matches

Black Outline: National cup (Copa del Rey) matches

Dark Grey: International cup (Europa League) matches

Different periodization alternatives have been effective in individual sports to solve this problem, searching for various fitness peaks during the season (Issurin & Kaverin, 1985; Bondarchuk, 1988; Touretski, 1998). These block periodization models have been based on the use of concentrated workloads, looking for a consecutive development of the physical capacities with an accumulated and residual effect in the training process (Issurin, 2008). The most extended representation of this kind of planning consists on the successive repetition of blocks with a determined orientation; Accumulation, Transmutation and Realisation, which are more commonly known as ATR models (Navarro, 2001; Issurin, 2010).

To date, very few football specific periodization models have been published (Miñano, 2006). Roca (2011) reported his experiences with F.C. Barcelona having based his periodization model on the studies of Solé (2006). In this case, uniform workloads were regularly applied during the season. Without doubt, it is a very interesting approach as it explains the workload distribution and organisation according to the phases of the season (preseason, competitions and regeneration) that this author established.

Tactical Periodization

One of the most recent innovative approaches to this topic has been called tactical periodization (Tamarit, 2007). This tendency has a special relevance after the success during recent years of Portuguese managers like José Mourinho and André Villas-Boas. Team organisation is the key factor of this training conception and from the first week of the season, training loads are directed towards this objective. Specific contents are sequenced during the season to allow a progression in the development of the game principles and sub-principles. The figure of Professor Vítor Frade is crucial to understand this reasoned football training methodology.

The publication of these kinds of studies (Miñano, 2006; Oliveira et al., 2007; Roca, 2011) has a value that cannot be estimated. They provide a theoretical explanation to models employed by very successful current elite managers, which helps to progress in the knowledge of the sport. The implementation of

strategies to accelerate recovery processes, prevent injuries and psychologically tolerate competition demands and its surroundings at the top level (mass media, supporters, etc.) takes a predominant place in these teams.

Top class footballers experience faster training adaptations than lower standard players so they can positively incorporate high cognitive demanding efforts almost from the initial phase of the pre-season. For instance, many of these teams are characterised by using specific high demanding loads from the first weeks of training. All these characteristic conditions of elite teams show that these training models should not be literally copied into lower level teams, but adapted to the particular idiosyncrasies of each of them.

During recent years, several personal studies (Mallo, 2011, 2012b) have examined the effect of applying a block periodization model in football teams with a lower competition density, with one match per week. This model was based on the use of varying workloads instead of the traditional linear ones, changing the direction of the stimulus in each training cycle. Although the starting point could be very similar to ATR models, the qualitative difference from them would be that players were not taken to such a high grade of fatigue, to allow them to take part and perform at their most in the weekly competition.

In the first of the studies (Mallo, 2011) the effect of this block periodization model was assessed in relation to performance in competition in a Spanish Division Two team during four consecutive seasons. Each season was divided into a series of training cycles which were further subdivided into three blocks, always following an identical order (Figure 11). The workloads of each block, which had a length of between two and four weeks, had a different orientation.

The first block was aimed at developing the capacity to carry out long duration high intensity exercises. Thus, a long intensive dynamic of efforts in practices (for more information about these kinds of practices, refer to Chapter 2) were a priority. The second block searched to increase the ability to perform repeated

maximum intensity exercises so short intensive practices were predominant. Finally, all the cycles concluded with a block that had the objective of adding the capacity to produce maximum intensity exercises so the training contents followed this dynamic of the efforts. This last block was less demanding than the previous ones, looking for

supercompensation or a tapering effect from the anterior work (Mújika & Padilla, 2003; Mújika, 2009). The training practices used in each of the blocks followed a preferential orientation in relation to the sequential structure of the cycles, although it never meant an exclusive hierarchy, as performance in football requires all these three types of components.

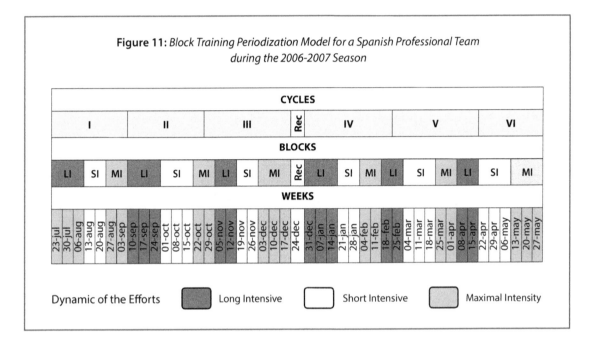

Figure 11: *Block Training Periodization Model for a Spanish Professional Team during the 2006-2007 Season*

The objective of the team during all four seasons of the study was to avoid relegation. This model was chosen proceeding from a basis that, with the same training dedication, the team with the best players would always finish in a higher position. For instance, given the fact that the actual team had one of the lowest budgets in the competition and that most of the teams usually adopt traditional periodization models, with linear workloads, an alternative strategy was selected. If what other teams did was repeated, team performance would be worse in comparison to those with better players.

All the training sessions carried out during the experimental period were recorded in computerised

forms, to allow calculating training times in each of the categories which were based upon the complexity and the dynamic of the efforts in the practices. The data analysis revealed significant differences ($P < 0.05$) in the workload orientation in each of the cycles, verifying that the theoretical statements that defined the model were respected.

To examine team performance in competition, the number of points obtained in each match (3 points per win, 1 point per draw, 0 points per defeat) was expressed in relation to the total number of points available, showing a final value of 47%. Interestingly, the highest success in competition was significantly ($P < 0.05$) greater in the third of the blocks, where 59%

Periodization Fitness Training

of the possible points were obtained, which was a higher score than that obtained in the first and second blocks. To try to reduce the effect that the standard of the opposition team might have had on this result, the teams were grouped according to their final league position into; top ranked (positions 1st to 6th), middle ranked (positions 7th to 13th) and bottom ranked (positions 14th to 20th). Again, the highest percentage of points was statistically (P < 0.05) obtained when confronting bottom and middle ranked teams in the third of the blocks (Figure 12).

It is important to highlight that all the training contents subjected to the periodization model referenced in this study were those organised by the fitness coach, representing between 31-34% of the total volume of the season. This distribution of

the training time is slightly different to what was recommended by Issurin (2008) in his block theory, where 60- 70% of the total volume was focused on two or three main objectives. As football requires a multi-factorial performance the approach to periodization was different than for individual sports. For instance, the actual model could be considered as accentuated workloads (Navarro, 2001), instead of concentrated, due to the fact that players were not induced to a maximal grade of fatigue as they had to compete every week.

Nevertheless, the fact that one third of total training time can help to direct the orientation seems very interesting. Although it may appear to represent a low percentage, it could reinforce Pareto´s principle, which is applied in economics and politics. This empirical

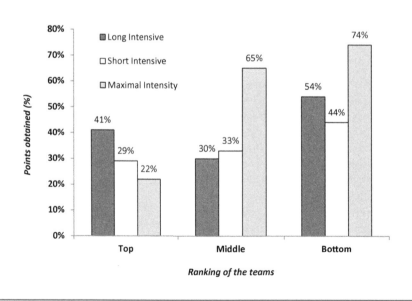

Figure 12: *Team Performance in Competition (Expressed as the Percentage of Points Obtained from the Total Number of Points Available) in Relation to the Opposition Team Final League Ranking in Each of the Blocks during 4 Seasons*

law, also known as the 80-20 rule, reflects how the majority of results (80%) are based on a minority of causes (20%). Even though the exact proportion is not so transcendent, applied to the present field it would point out the necessity of optimising training time. This law aims to achieve the greatest effects with the least energy usage. To be able to do so, it is essential to identify the key performance indicators to structure training around them.

In the second of the studies (Mallo, 2012b), the effect of applying the same accentuated block periodization model in different physical capacities relevant to physical performance in football was assessed during one season in a Spanish Division Two team. The influence of several programs on the development of different physical capacities has been previously examined (Helgerud et al., 2001; Hoff et al., 2002; Dupont et al., 2004; Gorostiaga et al., 2004; Wisloff et al., 2004; Stolen et al., 2005; Impellizzeri et al., 2006), although all these studies were carried out over short training periods of 8- 12 weeks. The experimental design of the actual study was very similar to the initial one, where five training cycles were further subdivided into three consecutive blocks. The evaluation of the physical capacities included a series of jumping tests on a contact platform, 10 yard sprint times using photoelectric gates and a level 1 yo-yo intermittent recovery test (Krustrup et al., 2003), where heart rate response was monitored during the exercise. These tests were carried out on the first session of each of the five cycles into which the season was divided. The results of the tests showed how explosive strength, acceleration capacity and the ability to perform long duration and high intensity intermittent exercises were maintained or improved during a 38 week competitive period.

As a practical example, the players covered 26-30% more distance in the high intensity running test at the end (training cycles four and five) than at the beginning (training cycle two) of the competitive period. The score in this test has been significantly related to the amount of high intensity distance covered during competition (Krustrup et al., 2003), so it could be expected that players had a better capacity to perform intense physical exercise in the final matches of the season. In addition, when team performance in competition (number of points obtained in relation to the number of points available) was examined during six Spanish Division Two consecutive seasons (2003-2004 to 2008-2009), it was observed that the percentage of points obtained in the last eight league matches was statistically greater ($P < 0.05$) than the season average.

When the results of both studies are interpreted together, one question which could arise is if varying workloads have a greater effect than linear workloads in football. In fact, it is well known that linear stimulation has induced to minor modifications, or even decrements, in conditional levels of several team sportsmen during the competitive period (Hakkinen, 1993; Schneider et al., 1998; Astorino et al., 2004; Kraemer et al., 2004; Gorostiaga et al., 2006). An additional advantage of the accentuated block periodization models, in relation to conventional ones, is that the cyclical organisation of training contents allows re-introducing injured players to team dynamics in a more progressive way.

It is undisputable that more investigations about the effect of this kind of periodization models in football are needed, even though they are very complicated to be carried out at elite level due to the number of variables that can affect the final outcome. The length of the competitive period and the fact of playing, at least, an official match per week do not recommend great fluctuations in team performance, which could apparently contradict what has been previously reported. The key in this case is to correctly dose the workloads to guarantee the recovery of players, avoiding confronting competition with a grade of fatigue that could affect team performance and increase the risk of sustaining injuries. The model described in the previous paragraphs has also been applied in another five seasons in teams where the aim was to win the league. In these cases, as teams presented a higher level inside the competition in which they took part, the number of points obtained in the matches was uniformly distributed during the season, with a need for consistent performances from the beginning to the end of the season to achieve the planned objectives.

The next stage in the development of this accentuated workload block periodization model was to integrate all the training practices in it. A methodological progression was elaborated, with the collaboration of the team manager Abraham Garcia, to work on the foundations of the team playing model and the tactical principles throughout the cycles and blocks into which the season was divided. Following this structure, the complexity and dynamic of the efforts in the practices were alternated to avoid the negative effect that regular workloads might have on performance. The richness of this design is greater as tactical training becomes the epicentre of periodization, requiring all the coaching staff to work on common objectives.

The introduction of intensive tactical and competitive practices was done early from the pre-season, without implicating an increase in the injury incidence, as footballers solve these situations relatively to their actual shape and, in extension, to their teammates and opponents shape. That is, a possession exercise would be carried out at a different absolute intensity in August than in November, but relative to the individual adaptation potential they can have a similar effect in both stages. The problem occurs when one of the players starts from a lower level than the other participants, either in August or November; this can turn into a greater risk of injury for this player as he is confronted by a more unstable environment.

Nevertheless, there is not a unique alternative to team training periodization and solutions adopted by coaches must depend on the analysis of each situation, based on the competition calendar. In top class teams, especially in those with a high competition density, the main part of the season is a repetition of an activation ->competition -> recovery loop, which makes it difficult going further from this linearity of workloads. Teams which take part in just one competition per week can design more creative strategies. The combination of both models cannot be ignored, starting with varied workloads in the early stages and then employing linear workloads during the competitive period. This way, the preparation period can be utilised to learn the basics of the playing model of the team, avoiding the use of generic workloads which are characteristic of traditional periodization models, and then look for successive adaptations to master the control of the game. Without doubt, this should be the final aim of all periodization models; to start the competition phase with high performances and improve them during the competition period.

To summarise this section, Figure 13 represents the theoretical evolution of the accentuated workloads periodization model during a season three-dimensionally. The horizontal axis shows the duration of the season and the succession of cycles (5) and blocks (3 colours; dark grey, white and light grey) in which it is subdivided according to the level of intensity in the dynamic of the efforts in the practices (long intensive, short intensive and maximum intensity, respectively). The vertical axis expresses the complexity of the tasks; as a new cycle starts the foundations from the previous one are reworked and new tactical contents are introduced. In this sense, the practices in each cycle have a greater level of complexity.

The interaction between both variables (z axis) shows the theoretical team performance level, understood as the capacity to play better, improving the richness of the competitive resources in the course of the season. Although the actual graphical illustration seems very rigid, it is important to remember that it will always be an open system which continuously offers new proposals according to the team and footballers´ adaptation levels.

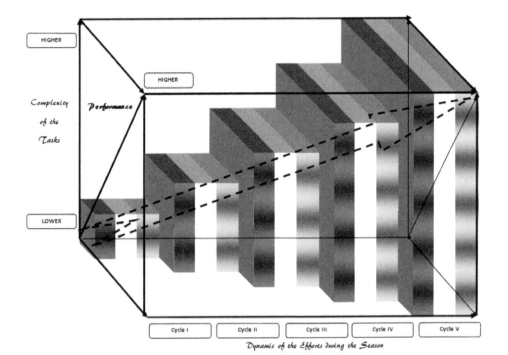

Figure 13: *Three Dimensional Accentuated Workload Block Periodization Model during a Season*

Predominance of the Dynamics of the Efforts in the Tasks:

Dark Grey = Long intensive
White = Short Intensive
Light Grey = Maximal Intensity

Periodization Fitness Training

3.2 MICRO-STRUCTURE OF PERIODIZATION

The micro-cycle is one of the most employed temporal units to organise training workloads and has a typical duration of between three and seven days (Navarro, 2001). In individual sports, micro-cycles have frequently been classified into adjustment, load, impact, activation, competition and recovery (Navarro, 2001). Seirul·lo (1987) and have provided an important conceptual advance for team sports after introducing the notion of a structured micro-cycle. The thinking of this author is based on a holistic conception of the footballer, where there is a continuous and dynamic interaction between all his structures, respecting the General Theory of the Systems. The structured micro-cycle can adopt different forms (preparatory, directed transformation, specific transformation, competitive and maintenance) depending if it is applied in the preparatory or competitive period. Furthermore, the type of training practices (generic, general, directed, specific and competitive) need to be adjusted to the moment of the season where they are used (Roca, 2011). In this book the duration of the micro-cycle has been related to the competition calendar. We take a team who periodically plays their competitive matches every Sunday as a reference, so the microcycle would be seven days long, although many variations could be found from this point on. If a team plays a matches one week on a Saturday and the next game on the following Sunday, the micro-cycle duration would be eight days.

On the other hand, if the match on a Saturday is followed by a game the next Wednesday and a third one on Sunday, two micro-cycles of four days would be established.

Re-taking the pattern of a team who repeatedly competes on Sundays, the beginning of the micro-cycle would be dedicated to psychological and physical match recovery. Normally, this phase occupies the initial 48 hour post-match period and is characterised by having a recovery session and a day off, or vice versa. The order in which these contents are organised depends on the manager's criteria and the analysis of each particular situation including travel, the players´ tiredness, the number of players that have not taken part in the previous match, etc. The same solution does not necessarily always have to be adopted, as the day where players are off can be changed during the weeks. It is essential to recognise that, approximately half of the players in the squad do not take part in each competitive match, so these players need to receive adequate stimulation in the two days directly after a match as they have not competed. This avoids them decreasing their performance level in relation to their teammates who played. Trying to keep all the players at the right level of training, attitude and performance is one of the most complicated duties when managing top class teams.

In the central part of the week (Wednesday and Thursday) the workloads aim to increase or maintain the capacities of the players, depending on the stage of the season the team is in. The practices should be focused towards features of the team organisation adapted to a specific dynamic of the efforts and, therefore, Sanz (2010) calls these days the structural phase. This is the stage which enables coaches a greater field of action. In professional teams with one match per week, two or three training sessions can be carried out in this phase. However, you need to respect that in some cases that players are not fully recovered from the previous match in the first of these sessions (for example, training on a Wednesday morning after having played on a Sunday evening, with a long journey back home after the game). Similarly, care must be taken with the first session after a day off, as an excessive intensity can increase the risk of injuries. In both cases, the stimulus needs to be progressively

planned and the practices could even be arranged into a morning and afternoon session. If the overall training workload of Wednesday is high, including a double session, the players can have Thursday morning off and resume training in the afternoon, to provide a better chance for recovery.

Exceeding the footballers´ tolerance limit in the central phase of the week does not make much sense, as it would negatively affect training quality, enhancing the likelihood of dragging fatigue to the next competitive match and increasing the chances of injuries occurring. Identical reasoning should be followed in the pre-competition activation phase (Friday and Saturday training sessions). This final stage must guarantee the assimilation, recovery and supercompensation of the work which has been carried out during the week, to reach competition in an optimum condition. Training in this phase can be oriented towards the situational factors (Sanz, 2010), reducing uncertainties in relation to the next opponent and preparing competition.

The higher the workload in the structural phase, the lower it should be in the situational phase to avoid competitive fatigue. For instance, in the case where players have over trained in the central part of the

week, Friday should ensure an active recovery. If the training workload employed on Wednesday and Thursday was tolerated by the footballers, training on Friday can continue with the same intensity.

Nevertheless, this final phase of the week requires increased recovery periods to avoid the development of cognitive and physical fatigue. Pre-match training days should be of short duration and should be used to reinforce the essential aspects of the team organisation towards the following day competition. The information has to be gradually transmitted during the week and, once you have reached this point, it is time to reinforce the major lines of action.

Finally, the micro-cycle concludes with the competition. In the case the match is played in the late afternoon or evening, a small activation session can be carried out in the morning, which can consist of a short walk, stretching and mobility exercises and even any kind of mental activation group games, to encourage cohesion and team spirit, or a low intensity tactical exercise (movements, set plays, etc.). Figure 14 represents a schematic overview of this seven day microcycle, showing the different phases into which it can be divided.

Figure 14: *Structure of a Seven Day Micro-cycle Which Includes One Competitive Match*

Recovery Phase		Development Phase		Activation Phase		Compe-tition
MONDAY	TUESDAY	WEDNESDAY	THURSDAY	FRIDAY	SATURDAY	SUNDAY
SESSION OR DAY OFF	DAY OFF OR SESSION	SESSION (1 or 2)	SESSION	SESSION	SESSION	MATCH

Applying this Micro-cycle to Non-Professional Teams

In non-professional teams, the interval between competitions is similar to the previous example although the number of training sessions during the week might differ. In any case, a recuperation phase (beginning), a development or maintenance phase (middle) and an activation phase (end of the week) can be structured. In these teams, the micro-cycle structure is often more conditioned by the availability of training grounds than by the desires of the coaches.

Professional Teams Competing in More than One Game a Week

A different reality takes place in professional teams playing more than one competitive match per week. In this case, the competition micro-cycles are rarely uniform. As an example, the competition period of Chelsea F.C. during the 2011-2012 season, from the first Premier League game of the season (August 14th) to the UEFA Champions League Final (May, 19th), has been used to illustrate these kind of teams. During this competitive period the team took part in 60 official matches from four different competitions (Premier League, FA Cup, League Cup and UEFA Champions League). Deducting the dates where the players were on international duty (with three quarters of the squad absent) the micro-cycles (period between two consecutive competitive games) could have been distributed in the following way:

How to Deal with Varying Micro-cycles at the Top Level

During the 2011-2012 season, Chelsea had twenty-two 3 day micro-cycles, thirteen 4 day micro-cycles, seven 5 days micro-cycles, seven 6 day micro-cycles and five 7 day micro-cycles.

Taking into consideration that the post-match recovery phase is at least 48 hours long and the pre-match activation phase lasts another 48 hours, objectives to develop the players´ capacities can only really be planned in a period of 6 days or longer. Hence, the majority of training drills/practices employed in the sessions of these teams are focused on detailed aspects of team functionality without

creating fatigue that cannot be tolerated by the players.

Interestingly, the teams that play the most games at the end of the season and achieve success are those who have best competed and not the ones that have trained the most. So in conclusion, competition turns out to be the most effective training component to improve team performance at the highest level.

Periodization Fitness Training

3.2.1 TRAINING LOAD DISTRIBUTION DURING THE MICRO-CYCLES

What is the optimal weekly training volume (in minutes)?

This is one of the most frequently asked questions by coaches. There is not a unique answer but it seems logical that the more a team competes, the less they should train and vice versa. In addition, the greater the quality of training, the lower quantity needed. Altogether, the question should not be how much training is necessary but how to train, ensuring the maximum quality in the practices which are used. This paradigm should be respected even in the pre-season; since intelligent, technical and fast players are required, the training practices should always be focused in this direction.

A universally accepted principle amongst coaches is the necessity to train in the same way that you wish to compete. It is possible that, in some cases, this notion has been misunderstood and it does not literally mean that the footballers need to train 90 minutes every day at their maximum physical intensity to achieve adaptations. A wider point of view is required, as not only the physical load of the training has to be monitored but, most importantly, the mental demands (concentration, application, strictness, seriousness) have to be considered. This training conception should lead to an education of the player to be able to maintain a maximum intensity of concentration during, at least, a 90 minute training or match duration (Mourinho, in Oliveira et al., 2007). For instance, training Specificity (Tamarit, 2007) does not imply the sole replication of competitive space and time parameters, but the adoption of a training style related to the team playing model.

If the volume and intensity of a competitive match are used as an arbitrary reference unit, one approach could be:

How many competition units should there be in a 7 day micro-cycle?

Built on the premise that a footballer who completes two competitive matches in a week is close to his tolerance limit, for those teams taking part in only one match per week, the volume of high demanding tasks should not exceed those additional 90 minutes. However, please note that you do not include the time used to explain the practices or during the transitions between them. The remaining on field training time during the week should be dedicated to warm ups, low intensity and extensive exercises.

This 90 minute volume (which is not an exact number and can have a wider range depending on each team) should be distributed into long intensive, short intensive and maximum intensity practices. From a practical point of view, 5-6 practices with 15 to 30 minutes duration each could be implemented during a week.

In order to prescribe work contents it is important to combine two classical training principles (Navarro, 2001) which could apparently seem contradictory. On one hand, the *Principle of Variety* reflects the necessity to alternate workloads to avoid the stagnation or regression of the sportsman. On the other hand, the *Principle of Repetition* is a request to set up conduct habits. Indeed, it is well known that the Central Nervous System learns from systematically repeating activities (Frade, in Díaz, 2012). These principles have been adapted by the tactical periodization theory (Oliveira et al., 2007; Tamarit, 2007). Thus, the *Principle of Horizontal Alternation in Specificity* recalls the need to vary the kind of stimulation during the micro-cycle. In addition, the *Principle of Propensities* aims to guarantee that certain behaviours are systematically repeated during sessions. This concept is intrinsically linked with what

Seirul·lo (in Roca, 2011) calls "preferential simulating situations", which would be conditioned tasks to help make sure that a certain kind of response repeatedly occurs, as only the intentional movement is educational. In a sense, the practices can be as the frames of a film sequence and need to be organised in a correct order to be meaningful. When they are designed in two dimensions on a sheet of paper they are only a declaration of intentions, but it is when they are carried out in the third dimension when they become relevant. Then we can see if they are able to trigger action and interaction conducts between the players.

On the basis of the previous principles, the workload variety, repetition and progression should be monitored to achieve the pretended effects. The time of exposure requires continuous adjustments; lengthening a stimulus on fatigued footballers is translated into training not being effective. If the tasks are very easy, the objective is quickly reached and variations are needed to avoid losing its sense. On other occasions, it happens in the opposite way as the designed practices are too complex for players. In these cases, they should be adapted and progressed from a more basic starting point. It should also be respected that well designed drills/practices sometimes do not have the optimum outcome on the field due to external factors that are not under the coach's control. If this was the situation, the coach has to be able to change the practice at the right moment, prioritising the collective benefit of the team above his personal ego.

In professional teams the drills/practices should be principally based on tactical and competitive levels of complexity, to cement the team playing model. In certain situations, due to a lack of human resources or training spaces, conditioning and technical practices can be used to increase the amount of intense exercise carried out by players, although these tasks involve a lower decisional component. If a team only has a small training space, the coaches would need to complement the small space drills with conditioning ones over longer distances, so they satisfy the physical requirements to prepare properly for competition. The same would happen in the opposite direction; if big spaces are always used, short intensive contents should be added to compensate weaknesses. All the conditioning contents should be carried out at the end of the session, so footballers can solve the complex tasks with the least fatigue possible.

The findings reported in the previous section could be extrapolated to micro-cycle periodization. Following this approximation, the workloads would be unevenly distributed during the week, aiming to achieve supercompensation in competition. Hence, the micro-cycle organisation would favour intensive exercises in the stimulation phase, with one session dedicated to long intensive conditioning and another to short intensive tasks. The sequence in which these two regimens are scheduled would depend on the recovery of the footballers from the proceeding match and on the tactical objectives to achieve.

Generally, as the player is not fully recovered on the first of these sessions (i.e., on a Wednesday after playing on a Sunday), short intensive drills are prescribed on this first day, whereas the second day is devoted to long intensive practices. Anyway, these stimulus do not have to always follow the same succession and could recreate the iterative method (Solé, 2006), varying their order during the week. The final part of the micro-cycle would be focused on active recovery and maximum intensity practices, to allow super-compensation from the previous work, trying to "refine" the competitive team performance. In addition to structuring the workloads in the microcycle, training contents need to follow an adequate chronology inside each collective on field training session, as indicated in the previous chapter. The warm up is used as an introduction and sets the methodological pathway of the session, linking it with the tactical and competitive objectives. Issues as to how the players are grouped inside the practices, marking the space, ball replacements or water breaks have to be clarified beforehand to reach a fluid transition between each practice, with every coach knowing their role.

Training Session 1 to follow shows an example of a training session in which practices are planned based on a tactical and competitive level of complexity and carried out in a long intensive dynamic of efforts.

Periodization Fitness Training

The sessions in which the practices are oriented towards a short intensive dynamic of efforts **(Training Session 2)** can be associated with a higher risk of sustaining traumatic injuries, due to the small spaces in which the players perform. Neuromuscular fatigue can also be elevated in these kinds of practices as the players perform more decelerations, accelerations, changes of directions and jumps, with the consequent eccentric muscular work and incidence of soft tissue injuries. Therefore, players need to be progressively introduced to these kinds of practices during pre-season to acquire a specific adaptation. If they are employed in isolation during training they can represent a risk, but if they are correctly managed and dosed, the muscular adaptations experienced by the players are much more powerful than any other gym content.

Finally, **Training Session 3** shows an example of a training session where the tactical and competitive objectives are executed in a maximum intensity dynamic of efforts. The overall duration of these sessions cannot be prolonged as doing so would go against the pretended benefits. As these practices are carried out in the final part of the week, previous to competition, the volume needs to be low to achieve an activation effect. Pre-match sessions can be complemented with team organisation low intensity or medium extensive practices.

TRAINING SESSION 1
Tactical and Competitive Practices for Long Intensive Dynamic Conditioning

INITIAL PART OF THE SESSION

Warm Up: Receive, Pass and Move Wheel   15 min

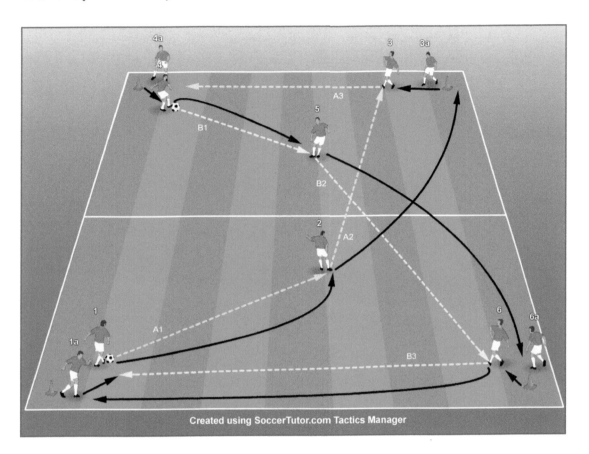

Created using SoccerTutor.com Tactics Manager

Description

The players work in groups of 10 players and we mark out a square as shown. There are 2 players in each corner and 2 players in the middle. The passing sequence is shown by the numbers.

The passing sequence starts with 2 balls simultaneously with Players 1 and 4. When Player 2and 5 receive the ball, they pass to Player 3 and Player 6 respectively. Players 3 and Player 6 then pass to the 2 players waiting (1a and 4a) who start the sequence again.

Each player follows their pass their pass so this practice works as a continuous sequence. At first the players pass with the hands and then progress to passing with feet.

Progressions

Increase difficulty: Play 1-2 combination with middle player or double pass on the sides, etc.

Activation: Pass + Sprint Exercise

5 min

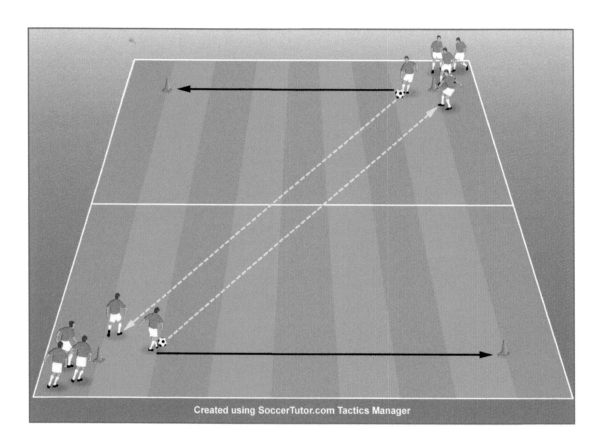

Description

Using the same area as the previous practice, we have 5 players in opposite corners as shown in the diagram.

2 players with the ball make a straight pass to the opposite corner simultaneously and then sprint to the cone to the right of them. Once every player has made their pass and sprinted to the cone, the players do the same again. The sequence continues until a full lap of the diamond/square is completed.

The players pass and sprint 4 times in a full lap. They then repeat another full lap in the opposite direction - pass and sprint to left.

MAIN PART OF THE SESSION

Tactical Shape and Positional Play in a 6 Goal 10 v 10 Game

30 min

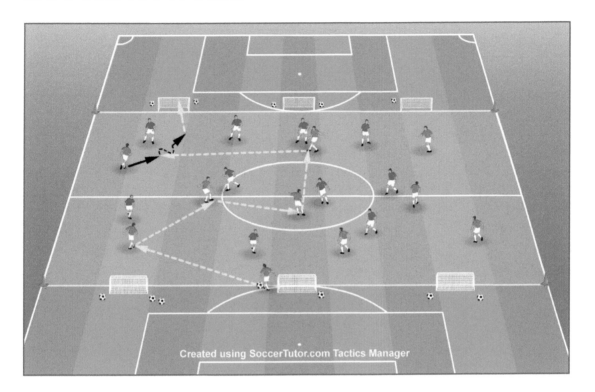

Created using SoccerTutor.com Tactics Manager

Attacking Tactical Objectives: Utilising width in attack, short/long passing game, pressing and winning the ball.

Defensive Tactical Objectives: Organisation, shape, pressing and quick collective reactions in the transition from attack to defence.

Description

2 teams play a tactical 10v10 game in the area shown and both teams defend and attack 3 small goals, each using a different formation. In this example, the blues are in a 4-4-2 formation and the reds are in a 4-3-3 formation.

We vary the conditions for each of the 3 sets. For example, in the second set, both teams have a goalkeeper support player behind the end line and in the third set the teams always finish in a different goal from where the play was started to encourage switching the play.

Volume: 3 sets of 8 minutes with 2 minutes recovery time after each set.

Positional Play, Crossing and Finishing in an 11 v 11 Dynamic Game

30 min

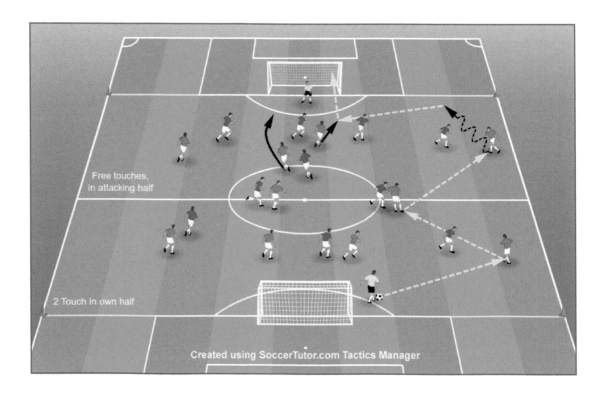

Free touches, in attacking half

2 Touch in own half

Created using SoccerTutor.com Tactics Manager

Description

Here we have the same principles as the previous practice and add 2 goalkeepers. We replace the small goals with 2 full sized goals on the edge of each penalty area and play an 11v11 game.

The players are limited to a maximum of 2 touches in their own half. In the attacking half, the players have unlimited touches.

A goal is worth double if it is scored from a cross from the wing.

Volume: 2 sets of 12 minutes with 3 minutes recovery time between sets.

FINAL PART OF THE SESSION: Stretching Exercises

TRAINING SESSION 2
Tactical and Competitive Practices for Short Intensive Dynamic Conditioning

INITIAL PART OF THE SESSION

General Warm Up - Running in 'Waves'   5 min

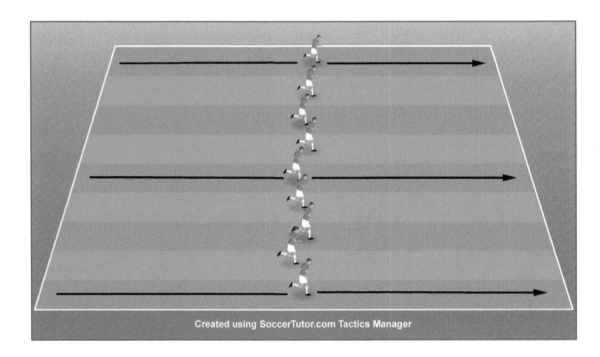

Created using SoccerTutor.com Tactics Manager

Objective

A warm up with general mobility exercises.

Description

This first exercise includes all the situations where the players move simultaneously in one direction. Vary the players movements with exercises such as normal jogging, running backwards, side-to-side, jumping up to head, short sprints + rest sequence etc.

It is a very basic type of warm up which can be carried out while moving around the field, from one penalty box to the other, using the width or half the length of the pitch.

Coaching Points

1. Include joint mobility exercises to open up the hips and shoulders in particular.
2. Make sure the players do their required stretches before, during or after this warm up exercise. Many players may have their own routine for this.

Specific Warm Up: Passing Exercises in Small Groups with 2 Balls

5 min

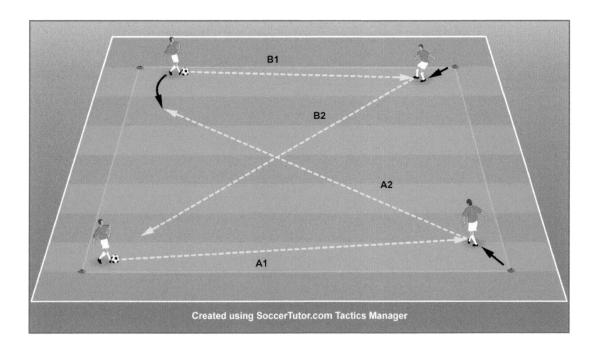

Created using SoccerTutor.com Tactics Manager

Objective

To develop the technique for passing and receiving, as well as awareness and timing during a warm up.

Description

We divide the players up into small groups of 4 and they work on this technical exercise within a small area. Each group of 4 players has 2 balls and simply pass the ball to each other using a maximum of 2 touches.

Coaching Points

1. Players should pass and receive with their back foot.
2. The players need to have their heads up to see the position of their teammates and the other ball when making a pass. Good awareness will create the right timing of passes to avoid any collisions of the 2 balls.

Activation: Rondo Possession Game

10 min

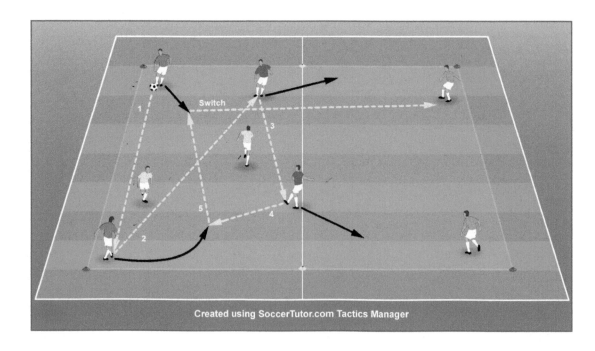

Objective

To develop passing, receiving, player movement and possession play in an exercise also intended to activate the muscles.

Description

We divide the team into groups of 8 players and mark out areas of 16 x 8 yards. Within each group, the players are divided into 4 pairs. The reds are positioned on the left, the blues in the middle, the oranges to the right and the yellows are the defenders.

On one side we have a rondo possession game with the players limited to 2 touches. 2 pairs aim to maintain possession against 1 pair (yellow in the diagram).

After completing 5 passes they have to play the other side (to an orange player). The blues and the yellows then move across to the other side to continue the same exercise on the right side. If a pair lose the ball, that pair switches roles with the 2 defenders.

Coaching Points

1. The speed of play needs to be high so the pass is played before angles are closed down.
2. The 2 defending players need to work together, pressing to block passing lanes.

MAIN PART OF THE SESSION

Short Intensive Dynamic Crossing and Finishing Passing Sequence

16 min

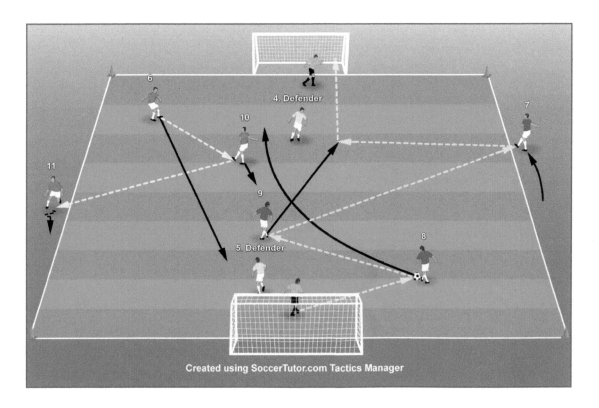

Created using SoccerTutor.com Tactics Manager

Attacking Tactical Objectives: Utilising width in attack and positional play.

Defensive Tactical Objectives: Positioning with lateral marking in the centre.

Description

In this practice, we mark out an area 30 x 20 yards and work with 2 defenders, 2 centre midfielders, 2 wingers, 2 forwards and 2 goalkeepers. The outfield players are divided into 2 groups of 3 and work simultaneously in opposite directions. The goalkeepers and defenders stay in one position.

Both goalkeepers start by passing to the centre midfielder who passes inside to the forward. The forward then passes out wide to the winger. The winger crosses the ball for the forward to finish and the defender tries to stop him. The same action is repeated consecutively 4 times with 2 in each direction.

Volume: 8 sets of 1 minute with 1 minute recovery time after each set (while the coach works with the 8 players in the other group). Vary the rules and sequence of passes.

Short Intensive 1v1 / 2v2 / 3v3 / 4v4
Dynamic Small Sided Games

16 min

In an area 30 x 20 yards, we have 8 outfield players (2 teams of 4) and 2 goalkeepers. We vary the amount of participants across 4 sets of different short intensive small sided games.

Attacking Tactical Objectives: Support play, creating space and 1v1/2v2/3v3/4v4 situations.

Defensive Tactical Objectives: Defensive covering and marking.

Set 1

We play 1v1 games (+GKs). The players are in pairs and take turns to play 20 second 1v1 duels. As soon as the first pair finish their 20 seconds, the second pair enter.

Each player plays 3 times and we play a total of 12 x 20 second games.

Set 2

We play 2v2 games (+GKs). The first 2 pairs play a 2v2 game for 40 seconds.

As soon as the first 2v2 game finishes, the 2 other pairs take their place to play a new 40 second 2v2 game.

Each player plays 4 games of 40 seconds with 40 seconds recovery time after each game (while outside). We play a total of 8 games.

Set 3

We play a 4v4 game (+GKs). We play 4 games that last 1 minute with 1 minute recovery time after each game.

Set 4

The players on the outside are all numbered (1-4). The coach calls out a number which relates to how many players will compete in the game.

Once they finish, they go back outside and the coach calls out a different number and we play again.

Change the players numbers so they get equal game time.

FINAL PART OF THE SESSION: Stretching Exercises

TRAINING SESSION 3
Tactical and Competitive Practices for Maximum Intensity Dynamic Conditioning

INITIAL PART OF THE SESSION

General Warm Up - Running in Squares   5 min

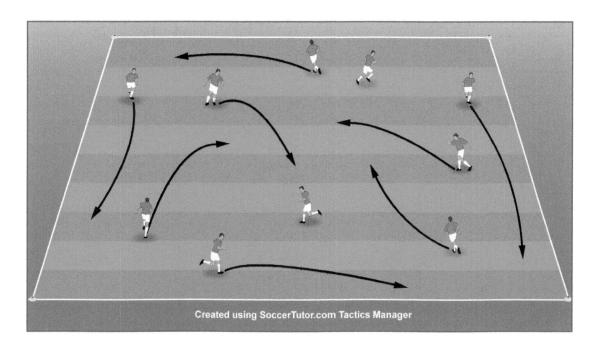

Created using SoccerTutor.com Tactics Manager

Objective

A warm up with general mobility exercises.

Description

This warm up is done within marked out squares. The size of the squares will depend upon the number of players. You can also group the players within different shapes such as rectangles, triangles or circles.

The difference to the previous warm up is that the players now move freely and with their own individually chosen trajectories inside the space, constantly changing direction.

Coaching Points

1. The players should use their run to attack the space.
2. Encourage the players to use changes of direction and different types of running i.e. side to- side running.
3. Make sure the players have their heads up and are aware of the players around them so they avoid collisions.

Specific Warm Up + Activation: Quick Passing & Applying Pressure

5 min

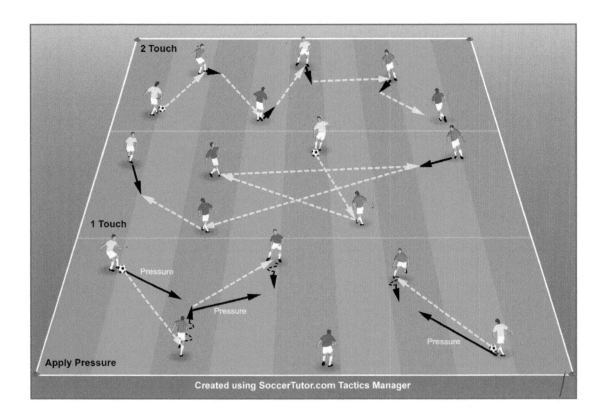

Created using SoccerTutor.com Tactics Manager

Description

In this practice we have 3 teams of 6 players (blue, red and yellow) with the players split into 3 pairs. The players are split into 3 sections as shown and progress through 3 different phases.

In the first phase the players pass the ball freely amongst each other and are limited to 2 touches and in the second phase they are limited to 1 touch.

Activation

5 min

Finally, in the third phase (activation), the players pass the ball to a different colour player and press the new ball carrier. The new ball carrier then does the same as shown.

In the final phase, once the player receives the ball and is pressed, he has to play a 1-2 combination with another player and runs round the pressing player to receive again.

MAIN PART OF THE SESSION

High Intensity Dynamic 3 Zone 6 v 3
Transitional Possession Game

24 min

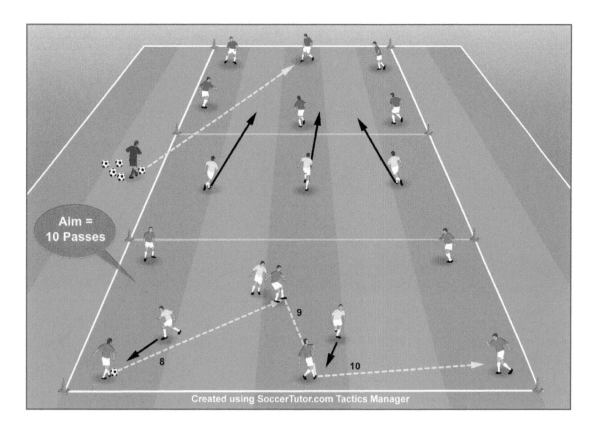

Attacking Tactical Objectives: Creating space, quick passing, support play and mobility.

Defensive Tactical Objectives: Fast organisation, pressing and closing passing lanes.

Description

In an area 45 x 15 yards, we have 3 teams of 6 players in 3 equal sized zones. We start in one end zone with a 6v3 situation with the team in possession limited to 2 touches. If they complete 10 consecutive passes, the coach plays a new ball to start the same situation at the other end. The 3 other yellow players move to apply pressure (6v3 again).

If a player loses the ball, the coach plays a new ball in to the other end and 3 players from that team move to apply pressure there and the other 3 move to the middle zone.

Volume: 3 sets of 6 minutes with 2 minutes recovery after each set.

Continuous High Intensity 7 v 7 (+6) Small Sided Games   24 min

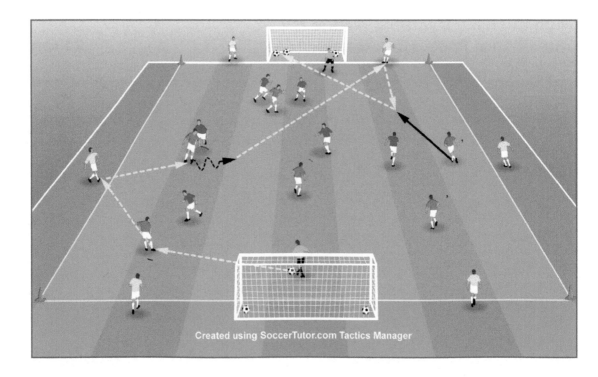

Created using SoccerTutor.com Tactics Manager

Attacking Tactical Objectives: Fast combination play, crossing and finishing.

Defensive Tactical Objectives: Applying pressure after losing the ball (transition from attack to defence).

Description

In an area 35 x 25 yards, we work with the same 3 teams as the previous practice and add 2 goalkeepers. 2 teams create a 7v7 situation inside the area and the other team are positioned outside, playing with the team in possession.

The first series is in the form of a league (6 x 1 minute play + 30 seconds recovery). The second series is the "king of the track" where the winning team remains and in the case of a draw, the team playing the longest moves to the outside.

Volume: 2 sets of 9 minutes with 2 minutes recovery time after each set.

＼ FINAL PART OF THE SESSION: Stretching Exercises

3.3 MONITORING THE TRAINING LOAD

Once the programmed training sessions have been put into practice it is important to store all relevant information regarding the collective (team) and individual (footballers) performance parameters.

This procedure should ensure the evaluation of the quality of the process, at the same time as allowing adjustments and providing a continuous system feedback. Data should be organised in a simple way so the coach can easily access them.

Figure 15 shows an example of a spreadsheet to record time employed in each of the drills/practice categories along successive micro-cycles, using the classification explained in the previous chapter.

Figure 15: *Training Volume (in Minutes) in Each of the Drill/Practice Categories during Successive Micro-cycles in a Professional Team*

Date	25	26	27	27	28	29	30	1	13-14	2	3	4	14	5	6	7	8	9	14-15	10	11	12	13	14	15	15	16	16	17	18	19	16
W-Up without ball	10	0	10	5	5	5	0	5	40	10	5	5	20	10	0	5	5	5	25	10	5	10	5	5	35	10	0	10	0	5	5	30
W-Up with ball	5	0	5	10	15	10	15	15	75	5	10	15	30	5	0	15	10	15	45	5	10	5	10	15	45	5	0	5	15	10	15	50
CONDITIONAL	20	0	0	15	0	0	10	10	45	20	5	0	25	10	0	0	10	0	20	20	0	10	5	0	35	20	0	0	10	0	0	30
Low Intensity	20								20	20			20	10					10	20					20	20						20
Extensive									0				0						0						0							
Long Intensive			15						15				0						0						0							
Short Intensive									0				0						0													
Maximal Intensity							10		10				5				10		10				10	5	15				10			10
TECHNICAL	0	0	20	0	0	15	0	0	35	20	0	0	20	20	0	15	0	0	35	30	10	15	0	0	55	20	0	15	10	0	0	45
Low Intensity									0	20			20	20					20	30					30	20						20
Extensive			20		15				35				0			15			15		10	15			25			15	10			25
Long Intensive									0				0						0						0							0
Short Intensive									0				0						0						0							0
Maximal Intensity									0				0						0						0							0
TACTICAL	20	0	25	25	45	25	25	0	165	0	40	0	40	10	0	30	35	0	75	0	20	25	20	0	65	10	0	25	30	25	0	80
Low Intensity	20						10		30		10		10	10		15	20		45				20		20	10			15	10		35
Extensive			25		15	25			65		20		20			15			15		20	25			45			25	15	15		55
Long Intensive				30					30				0						0						0							0
Short Intensive				25					25				0						0						0							0
Maximal Intensity						15			15				10				15		15						0							0
COMPETITIVE	0	0	20	25	30	25	15	0	115	0	0	0	0	0	0	20	0	0	20	0	20	20	15	0	55	0	0	15	20	15	0	50
Low Intensity									0				0						0						0							0
Extensive									0				0						0		20				20							0
Long Intensive			20		30				50				0			20			20			20			20				20			20
Short Intensive				25					25				0						0						0			15				15
Maximal Intensity					25	15			40				0						0				15		15					15		15

Periodization Fitness Training

Several technological applications have been released into the market recently to help, although, as it is a very dynamic process, individual solutions that all management staff can develop are usually more functional than closed computerised software. Coaches should possess their own training quality control system, which needs to be complemented with competitive team performance indicators.

The use of control sheets, as the one shown in Figure 15, present the utility of estimating the training load experienced by footballers in the course of a certain period. Since there are plenty of factors that might impact it, it is very complicated to have a unique measurement of the overall training workload. Different parameters have been employed during the last years to determine the external (distance covered, high-intensity activities, accelerations, decelerations, metabolic power, etc.) and internal (heart rate, lactate, hormonal concentration in saliva, etc.) workloads that footballers are subjected to. The training workload concept should not be limited to the collection of these conditional and physiological parameters, but

complemented with data related to the complexity of the drills planned during the session. In this sense, scales based on the subjective perception of effort have proven to be effective indicators of training demands (Impellizzeri et al., 2004; Abrantes et al., 2012; Casamichana et al., 2012).

Another non-invasive alternative to quantify the training load is the development of scales based on the kind of drills employed during the sessions. In this case, results are expressed in relation to competition demands, which in this example would have a value of 10 points (maximum score). Thereafter, each of the training categories (Figure 15) would receive a value depending on their complexity and dynamics of the efforts. Once the session has finished, the time (in minutes) that the team has performed each practice is multiplied by the workload index. The sum of all the drills used during a session can allow estimating the training load of that day. Figure 16 illustrates this kind of representation after studying the workload evolution for a player during several successive competitive period microcycles.

Figure 16: *Estimation of the Training Workload of a Footballer during Successive Micro-cycles in a Professional Team*

	C1 (5)					C2 (7)							C3 (6)						C4 (4)				REC1 (4)			
	13	14	15	16	17	18	19	20	21	22	23	24	25	26	27	28	29	30	31	1	2	3	4	5	6	7
Training Sessions	2	1	1	1		1		2	1	1	1		1		2	1	1		1	1	1					
Matches					1							1						1				1				
Days Off							1							1									1	1	1	1
Volume (min)	140	100	75	100	115	70	0	135	110	85	75	115	85	0	130	100	60	115	90	80	55	115	0	0	0	0
Work Load	5,2	4,5	4,1	3,2	10	3,8	0	7,1	4,9	3,1	2,3	10	4,4	0	6,1	4,2	2,5	10	4,9	3,7	1,8	10	0	0	0	0

To allow establishing methodological progressions of increasing complexity it is essential to record all the practices employed during each session on a day-to-day basis. This also facilitates a better sequencing of the principles and sub-principles of the playing model during the season and in the phases into which they are divided. The faster the players absorb tactical knowledge should mark the evolution and aid in

reaching higher difficulty levels when planning the practices. This information must always be completed with that extracted from competition, which is the real test of the team and footballers´ tactical competence. Continuous adjustments of the training and competition loop should lead to qualitative improvements of the team performance during the season.

Monitoring physical parameters during training and competition can help get additional information to enrich the process interpretation, but always respecting that they are only referring to one (conditional) dimension of performance, so they should be complemented with technical and, specially, tactical analysis to provide an integral map of the scenario.

Furthermore, having a library of training practices can be of great help to determine the exact demands that each of them usually represents. Each coach is guided by his own experience to choose certain kinds of drills/practices which have proven effective in the past to achieve his objectives, letting the players learn the concepts he wants to transmit. The flexible adaptation of these practices to every specific context helps reduce the uncertainty of the process.

At the same time as monitoring the team performance, each footballer must be analysed within each session. In this case, it is interesting to control the individual diary training workload, not forgetting about the pre and post training exercises.

Figure 17 (on the next page) provides an example of the load experienced by a player calculated after registering time employed in each of the practices. Therefore, not all the footballers in a team present the same workload at the end of the day or the end of a micro-cycle, as they do not necessarily carry out the same practices during each session. In addition, this kind of control allows prescribing individual training practices according to each training period and developing specific injury prevention programs, to reduce the occurance of nontraumatic injuries (Paredes, 2009).

Figure 17: *Monitoring the Individual Workload of a Professional Footballer during a Training Cycle*

	PLAYER										CYC
	1	2	3	4	5	6	7	8	9	10	I
Training Sessions	4	10	5	7	6	4	5	6	7	0	54
Matches	0	0	0	0	0	0	1	1	2	0	4
Day Off	0	0	3	1	1	3	1	1	0	4	14
Volume (min)	275	785	480	540	495	355	600	605	745	0	4880
Work Load	11,6	33,1	27,9	27,5	29,9	19,4	30,8	31,8	43,2	0	225
PRE-SESSION	**0**	**60**	**25**	**20**	**0**	**0**	**60**	**95**	**75**	**0**	**335**
Bike		5	20				20	25	15		85
Pre-Activation		15	5				40	40	30		130
Strength		40		20				30	30		120
SESSIONS	**275**	**725**	**445**	**520**	**495**	**355**	**540**	**510**	**670**	**0**	**4545**
W-Up without ball	**10**	**65**	**45**	**50**	**45**	**25**	**30**	**35**	**40**	**0**	**345**
Waves	5	25	10	10	15	10	5	10	5		95
Squares		10	5	15			5		5		40
Lines	5		20	10	15	15	5	15	10		95
Games			5								5
Activation		30	5	15	15	0	15	10	20		110
W-Up without ball	**0**	**70**	**70**	**60**	**55**	**35**	**60**	**50**	**95**	**0**	**495**
Small Groups		25	25	25	20	15	20	15	25		170
Squares		5	20	10	10	10	10	10	20		95
Passing Seq.		5		10	10		15	10	10		60
Games		35	15						20		70
Tactical			10	5	10	10	15	15	15		80
			10	5					5		20

EPILOGUE

Many approaches can be followed to develop a structure, organisation and methodology of football training and, for instance, during the previous pages a reflection about one of the possible alternatives has been presented. There is no doubt that each coach should build their own way based on the ideas they get from one place or another, and at the same time combine them with their own practical experiences. The interaction between theory and practice is critical to progress a coach's knowledge.

As a result of everything addressed in the previous 3 chapters, Figure 18 summarises the thinking line followed in this book, representing the foundation of the training process. It is again essential to reinforce that it is an open, adaptable, chaotic, complex, dynamic and evolving system, so nothing of what was previously exposed should be considered as an absolute truth, as every team and every player requires a personalised approach.

Even more, in a short space of time, the ideas reflected here would probably be obsolete and new perspectives would pave the way to more elaborated interpretations of the object of study. The footballer and the ball have to be always moving, as well as the theory and practice of football training.

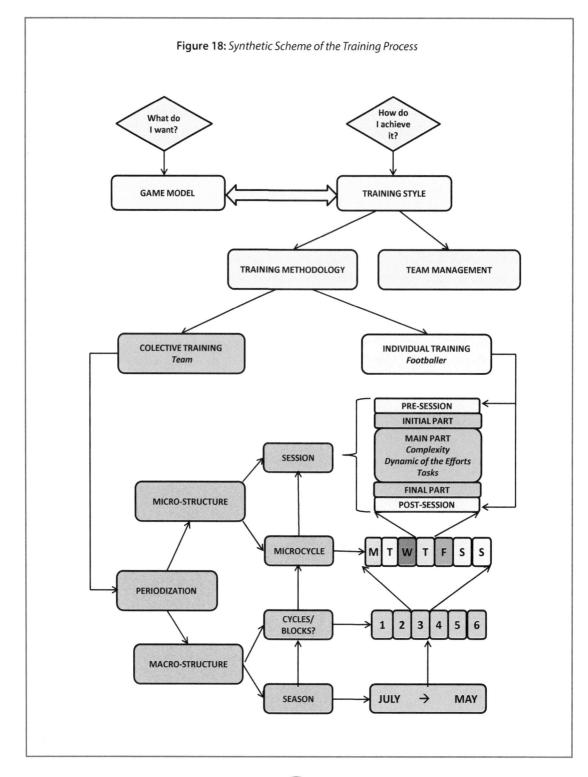

Figure 18: *Synthetic Scheme of the Training Process*

CHAPTER 4

TRAINING SESSIONS FOR THE 4 PHASES OF THE GAME

TRAINING SESSIONS FOR THE 4 PHASES OF THE GAME

All the sessions are organised following the same criteria that has been explained in the previous chapters of this book.

The first aim of the training session is to be in accordance with the playing model of the team and, thus, all sessions must follow a tactical objective. To do so, four different kind of sessions have been designed as examples, one for each of the main phases of the game (attack, defence, transition attack-defence, and transition defence-attack). As they are general examples, the peculiar characteristics of the team and the next team to be confronted in competition, have not been taken into consideration.

Once selected the tactical objectives, a prioritised effort dynamics was chosen. During the competition period, the sessions are focused on a long intensive, short intensive, or maximal intensity dynamic of the efforts. Thus the number of players, spaces, durations, are rules of the drills are modified according to the aims pursued and, specially, to the level of the players involved. There is not a generic rule in this sense, so these parameters have to be individually adjusted to each specific training scenario.

TRAINING SESSION 4
Long Intensive Attacking Practices

INITIAL PART OF THE SESSION

Warm Up: Double Passing Square - Short & Long Support Play with Directional Touches

10 min

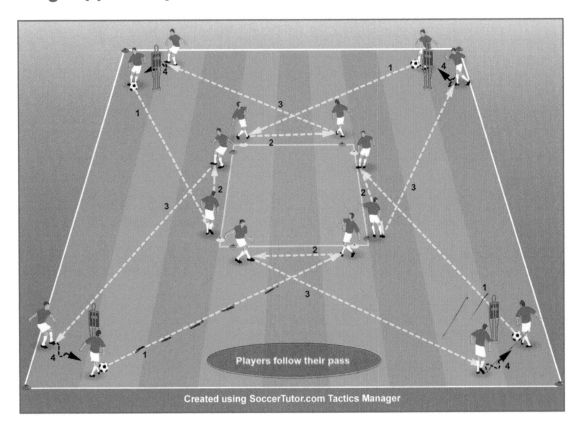

Players follow their pass

Created using SoccerTutor.com Tactics Manager

Description

We mark out an outside square of 15 x 15 yards (with 1 mannequin in each corner) and an inside square of 10 x 10 yards. We play with 4 balls at the same time.

The players always pass and move following the same sequence; diagonal ball inside, set the ball for the next player and then a diagonal ball outside. This sequence is continuously repeated.

Variations

1. Start with the players dribbling the ball, then progress to pass and move.
2. After every pass, get the players to do an individual warm-up exercise.
3. Change the direction of play every 2 minutes
4. Increase the difficulty with extra 1-2 combinations in the corners behind the mannequins.

Activation - Dribbling Relay Runs　　　　　　5 min

Use the 4 corners of the bigger square from the previous practice and run relays. The first player in each corner dribbles the ball to the opposite corner until completing the lap. Variations can include; dribble and pass; pass and sprint.

Warm Up: 3 v 3 (+2) Support Play in a 3 Zone Possession Game　　15 min

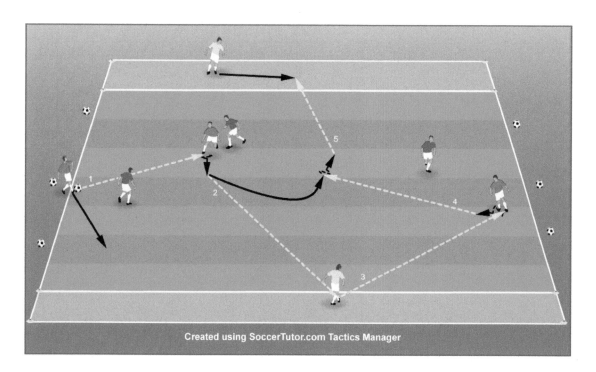

Created using SoccerTutor.com Tactics Manager

Description

In a 20 x 15 yard rectangle, we split the players into groups of 8 and play possession games. In each group we have a 3v3 situation inside the rectangle and 2 neutral players (yellow) in small zones on the long side who play with the team in possession. The inside players are limited to 2 touches and the neutral players have 1 touch.

If the players' usual position is in the centre (centre back, centre midfielder or forward) they work on the long side of the rectangle. When the neutral players are full backs or wingers, create a small zone on the short side of the rectangle.

Volume: 3 sets of 4 minutes with 1 minute recovery time after each set.

MAIN PART OF THE SESSION

Building Up Play, Maintaining Possession in the Centre and 11 v 4 Attack

15 min

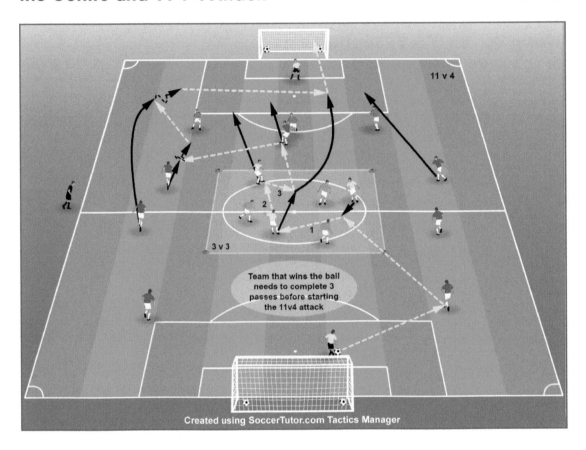

Description

Using a full pitch, we mark out a 15 x 15 yard square in the middle with 6 players inside (2 teams of 3 players - orange and yellow). All players are in their specific positional roles. The goalkeeper starts with the ball which then has to be played into the central square.

Both groups of 3 players fight for the ball and then aim to complete 3 consecutive passes inside the square to become part of the attacking team with the blue players (11v4) and attack the other goal. There are 3 defenders (red) and a goalkeeper who defend the goal. The 3 players in the central square wait until the next play starts.

Variation

The full backs and wide midfielders support outside the square to help keep possession.

Volume: 2 sets of 7 minutes with 1 minute recovery time between the sets.

Possession, Direct Play and Match Scenarios in a Dynamic Competitive 9 v 9 SSG

36 min

Created using SoccerTutor.com Tactics Manager

Description

Using the area in between the 2 penalty areas and 2 full sized goals, we play a 9v9 game with different conditions.

Change the focus and objectives for each of the 3 sets:

Set 1: Focus on possession football involving as many players in the build up play as possible. The diagram shows this example as the red team keep the ball well, switch the play and then move inside again to score.

Set 2: Change the focus to direct football (long balls) with the aim to get from back to front very quickly.

Set 3: Play a game scenario - It is the last 10 minutes of a competitive game and one team is 1-0 down. That team must work under competitive constraints to try and score a goal.

Volume: 3 sets of 10 minutes with 2 minutes recovery time after each set.

FINAL PART OF THE SESSION: Stretching Exercises

TRAINING SESSION 5
Short Intensive Defensive Practices

INITIAL PART OF THE SESSION

Coordination, Resistance & Speed of Footwork Exercise

10 min

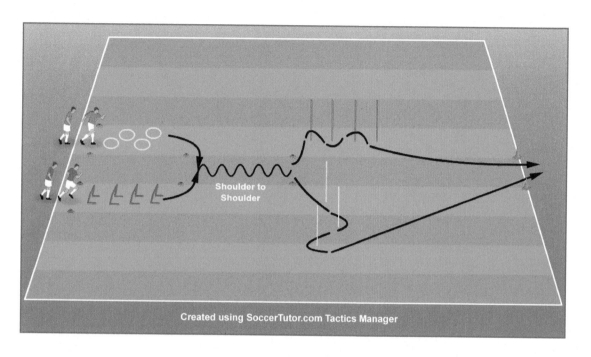

Shoulder to Shoulder

Created using SoccerTutor.com Tactics Manager

Objective

To develop speed, acceleration, coordination and strength in a warm up.

Description

Divide the players into 2 lines and position the speed rings, hurdles and poles as shown.

2 players start at the same time and perform a coordination exercise (footwork pattern speed rings/jump over small hurdles), then meet each other and move forward while pushing shoulder to shoulder to the cone. Once they separate, they run through the poles (different movement patterns), then change pace (sprint) to final cone and jog back.

Activation

5 min

Using the same exercises (or change coordination exercises to ladders, sticks) and complete the sequence at maximum intensity, but walk back at the end instead of jogging.

MAIN PART OF THE SESSION

Speed, Acceleration and Defending the Goal in a 1 v 1 Duel

14 min

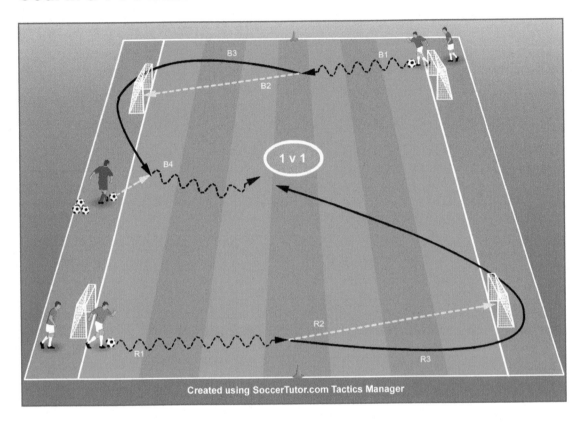

Created using SoccerTutor.com Tactics Manager

Objective

To develop the quick movements and acceleration to defend in 1v1 duels.

Description

In an area 20 x 25 yards we position 4 small goals as shown. The players are in 2 lines in opposite corners and 2 players start at the same time, dribbling the ball forwards.

The players shoot in the small goal opposite and then sprint around the goal. Once they have gone around the goal, the coach plays a ball to one player and they then compete in a 1v1 duel. The player defends the 2 goals on their side to prevent a goal.

Set 1: 1v1 duels.
Set 2: 2v2 duels. The players start in pairs from the 4 corners.

Volume: 2 sets of 6 minutes with 1 minute recovery time after each set.

Defend the Goal in a 2 v 2 Shooting Practice

12 min

Recovery Zone   Recovery Zone

Created using SoccerTutor.com Tactics Manager

Objective

We work on defending the goal, which includes closing the passing lanes and short intensive training with fast movements (front, back, sideways).

Description

In an area 20 x 10 yard area, we place 2 small goals on the short sides of the area. The players are in groups of 8 players. 4 players work while 4 players are recovering.

The area is divided into 4 equal zones with 1 player inside each section. The players are in pairs and one team has the ball. The attacking team (blue) are limited to 2 touches and try to score in the opposition's goal.

Both defenders (red) of the same team have to work together on defensive concepts (closing passing lanes) and on short and fast movements (front, back, sideways).

Volume: 6 sets of 1 minute work with 1 minute recovery time after each set.

Continuous 1v1, 2v2 , 3v3, 4v4 Duels Circuit　　　36 min

1st min (Player 1's) = 1v1
2nd min (Player 2's) = 2v2
3rd min (Player 3's) = 3v3
4th min (Player 4's) = 4v4

The sequence is repeated in the opposite order. See description

Created using SoccerTutor.com Tactics Manager

Description

In an area 35 x 30 yards, we have 2 teams of 4 players + 2 goalkeepers. Players from each team are numbered (1 to 4) and follow a sequence.

The practice starts with a 1v1 situation for 1 minute. In the 2nd minute, 1 player from each team comes in (2v2). In the 3rd minute, 2 more players come in (3v3), and 2 more in the 4th minute (4v4).

The sequence is then repeated in the opposite order as the players who started come out after 1 minute (3v3), another 2 after another 1 minute (2v2) and another 2 after another minute as we finish as we started with a 1v1 duel. Each set is 7 minutes long.

The second, third and fourth sets are started with players numbered in a different order.

Volume: 4 sets of 7 minutes with 2 minutes recovery time after each set.

FINAL PART OF THE SESSION: Stretching Exercises

TRAINING SESSION 6
Maximum Intensity Practices for the Transition from Attack to Defence

INITIAL PART OF THE SESSION

Quick Movements, Aerial Control and Passing Warm Up

10 min

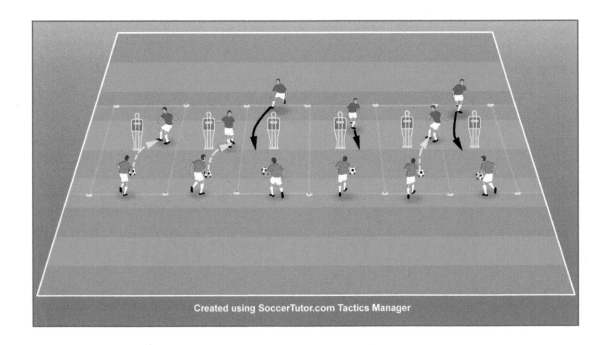

Created using SoccerTutor.com Tactics Manager

Objective

To develop quick movements, footwork, aerial control and passing in a warm up.

Description

Players are in pairs with 1 ball and a mannequin in between them. One player (red) throws the ball and the other sprints round the mannequin to receive.

The red player plays it back in different ways:

1. Inside of the foot volley pass.
2. Instep or laces volley pass.
3. Players take 2 touches; chest + inside of foot volley, thigh + instep volley pass, etc.
4. Headed pass.

Change the roles of the red and blue players so they get equal time for both parts.

Variation

Change the type of movements (front, back, sideways, jumps) and passing combinations.

148

Periodization Fitness Training

Activation: Short Sprints, Quick Reactions and Switching Positions

5 min

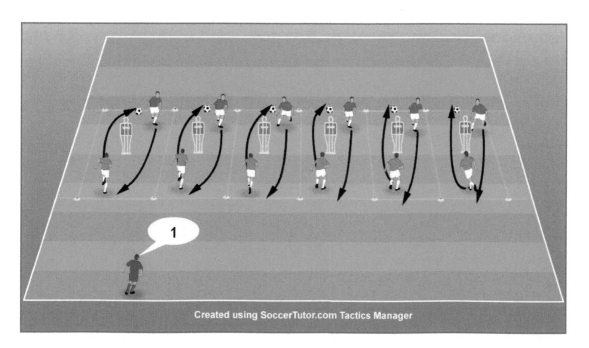

Created using SoccerTutor.com Tactics Manager

Objective

To develop quick movements, acceleration and explosive power.

Description

This practice is very similar to the previous one with the players again in pairs and in the same area with the mannequins.

This time the players do not use the ball and they both work at the same time. If the coach calls out "1" both players have to switch positions in a clockwise direction. If the coach calls out "2" the players have to switch positions in an anti-clockwise direction.

Variations

1. The coach can use different commands (letters, words, get the players to do the opposite of what is said or even use visual signals to improve awareness).
2. The players can take up different starting positions such as facing the mannequins, back to back to the mannequins, etc.

Periodization Fitness Training

MAIN PART OF THE SESSION

Transition from Attack to Defence in Simultaneous Dynamic 4 v 2 Rondos

18 min

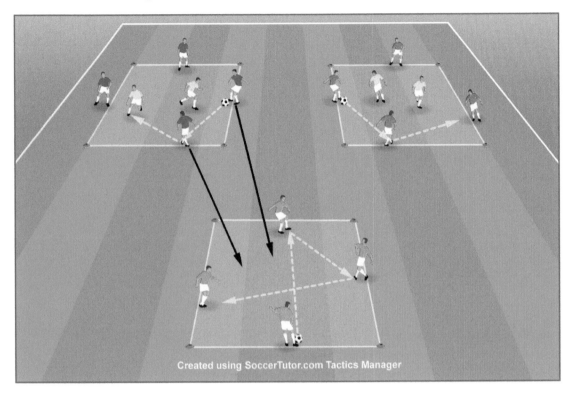

Created using SoccerTutor.com Tactics Manager

Description

We mark out 3 squares of 8 x 8 yards as shown, with 10 yards distance between them. 4 players are positioned on one side of each square and 2 players defend inside trying to win the ball (4v2 possession exercise). One square has no defenders.

The defending players try to touch the ball and if they do, the player who missed the pass and the one that made the previous pass (the 2 blue players in the diagram) then become the defenders and have to go to defend in the third square.

Variations

1. All the players are limited to 2 touches.
2. Alternate between the players being allowed 1 or 2 touches.
3. All the players are limited to 1 touch.
4. If 4 players complete 10 consecutive passes, the same defenders then have to go to defend in another square.

Volume: 3 sets of 5 minutes with 1 minute recovery time after each set.

150

Periodization Fitness Training

Position Specific Circuit Training with Combination Play, Finishing & 2 v 1 Attack

15 min

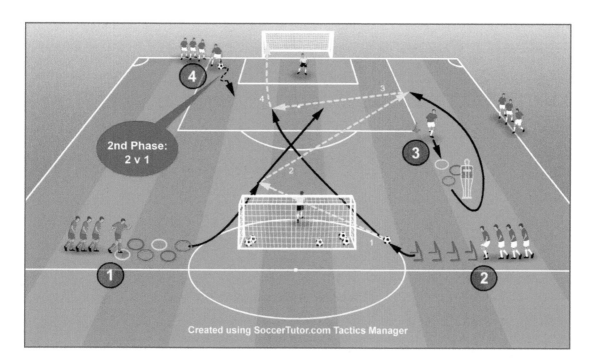

Created using SoccerTutor.com Tactics Manager

Description

Using half a full sized pitch, we have players in 4 positional roles.

2 players (red defender + blue attacker) start at the same time from one end and perform a coordination exercise (footwork). Player 3 starts facing the opposite way, performs a coordination exercise and changes direction round the mannequin.

Player 2 passes inside to Player 1 who plays the ball out wide to Player 3 (full back or winger). Player 3 crosses the ball for either of the other 2 to finish on goal.

As soon as they finish, another player starts from the other corner to start a 2v1 attack with Player 2. The defensive player (Player 1 in red) now becomes the defender.

Variations for the 2nd Set

1. Change the direction of the exercise so the cross comes from the opposite side.
2. Change the footwork patterns - can use ladders or sticks.

Volume: 2 sets of 7 minutes with 1 minute recovery time in between the 2 sets.

Maximum Intensity 3 Zone Dynamic Transition Game ⠀⠀⠀ *24 min*

40 x 50

Created using SoccerTutor.com Tactics Manager

Description

Mark out an area 40 x 50 yards as shown and divide it into 3 sections. The 2 end zones are 40 x 18 yards. There are 2 teams of 8 players + 2 goalkeepers. 4 players from each team work at a time while the other 4 are recovering. This ensures maximum intensity.

The practice starts with the goalkeeper and a 4v4 situation in one end zone. The players aim to keep possession with the goalkeeper acting as a neutral player who plays with the team in possession. When that team loses the ball, the other team can quickly attack the opposite goal. The team that had the ball has to react quickly to defend (transition).

The sequence starts again in the opposite end zone with the other team this time. After every 2 sequences, the players swap with those waiting outside for recovery time.

Volume: 3 sets of 6 minutes with 2 minutes recovery time after each set.

FINAL PART OF THE SESSION: Stretching Exercises

TRAINING SESSION 7
Long Intensive Practices for the Transition from Defence to Attack

INITIAL PART OF THE SESSION

Technical 3 Player Combination Warm Up with Timing of Forward Runs

10 min

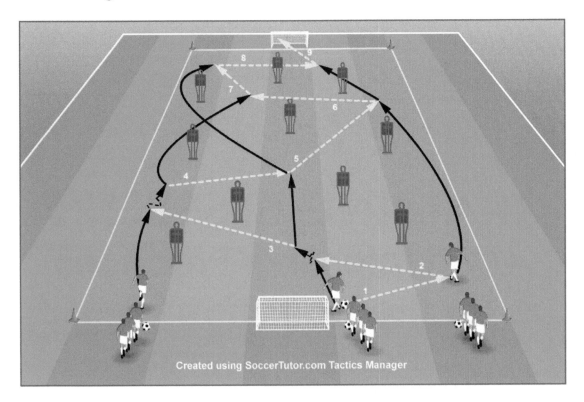

Created using SoccerTutor.com Tactics Manager

Objective

To develop attacking combinations and the timing of forward runs in a warm up.

Description

In an area 40 x 20 yards we have 1 small goal at each end. Players in groups of 3 pass the ball between each other, making runs behind/around the mannequins (defenders). They finish their attacking combination play by finishing in the opposite goal. When all the groups finish, they start in the opposite direction with the same objectives.

Variations

1. Use groups of 4 players for more complicated attacking combinations.
2. All the players are limited to 2 touches.
3. All the players are limited to 1 touch.
4. The players have to finish the attack within 6-8 seconds.

154

Activation: Global Speed and Power Circuit

5 min

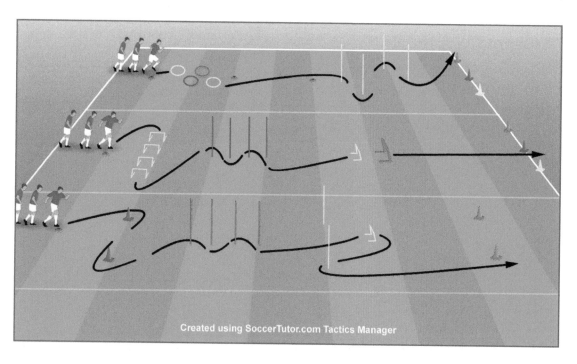

Created using SoccerTutor.com Tactics Manager

Objective

To develop speed, acceleration, agility, strength and power.

Description

The players are in 3 lines as shown, with various different coordination exercises with speed rings, hurdles and poles.

1. Hop through speed rings, sprint, change direction through the poles and sprint to the cone at the end.
2. The players jump over 4 small hurdles, slalom through the poles, jump 1 small hurdle + 1 high hurdle, and then finally sprint to the end cone.
3. The players run round the cones as shown, slalom through the poles, sprint + jump over small hurdle, change direction round the pole and sprint to the end cone.

Volume: The players perform 6 repetitions each (2 of each exercise).

Variations

1. When changing direction through the poles, the players should slow down, bend their knees and then push off one foot to accelerate in the opposite direction.
2. Balance is very important when transferring from one leg to the other through the rings.

Periodization Fitness Training

MAIN PART OF THE SESSION

Press and Win the Ball in a 2 v 4 / 10 (+2) v 4 Double Square Possession Game

15 min

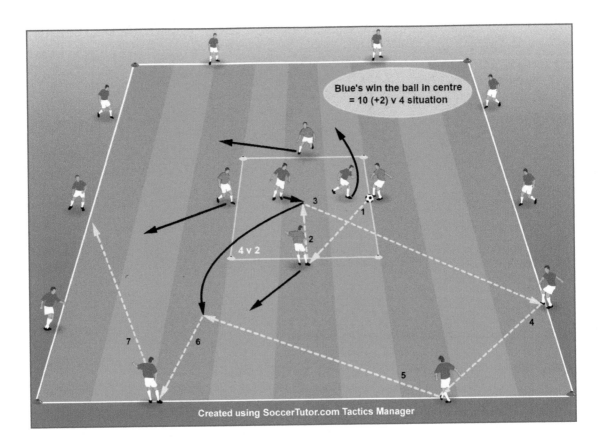

Blue's win the ball in centre = 10 (+2) v 4 situation

4 v 2

Created using SoccerTutor.com Tactics Manager

Description

In an area 30 x 20 yards, we mark out an 8 v 8 yard square in the middle as shown.

The practice starts with a 4v2 situation in the central square. When the 2 blue players win the ball, they can then play it to one of their 10 teammates on the outside and it becomes a 10 (+2) v 4 situation in the whole 30 x 20 yard area. When the blues lose the ball, the practice starts again within the 4v2 small square.

Variations

1. Change the positions of the players after each set.
2. The players are limited to 1 or 2 touches.

Volume: 3 sets of 4 minutes with 1 minute recovery time after each set.

156

Periodization Fitness Training

Counter Attack in the Centre in a 7 v 9
Transition Game with 3 Goals

20 min

Created using SoccerTutor.com Tactics Manager

Objective

We work on keeping possession, pressing and fast break attacks from the centre.

Description

We mark out a 50 x 40 yard area in the centre of the of a full sized pitch as shown. There are 2 teams and there is a 9v7 situation. The 9 players try to keep possession and every time they complete 10 consecutive passes they get 1 point.

The defending team try to win the ball and when they do, they play the ball outside the area and 1 player can attack any of the 3 goals (transition from defence to attack).

As soon as the ball is played out, the coach plays another ball in immediately so the players inside the square are always active. Change the roles of the teams for the second set.

Variation

2 players can go outside the area and they have to perform a cross and finish.

Volume: 2 sets of 8 minutes with 2 minutes recovery time after each set.

Fast Transition to Attack in a 9 v 9 Zonal Small Sided Game

30 min

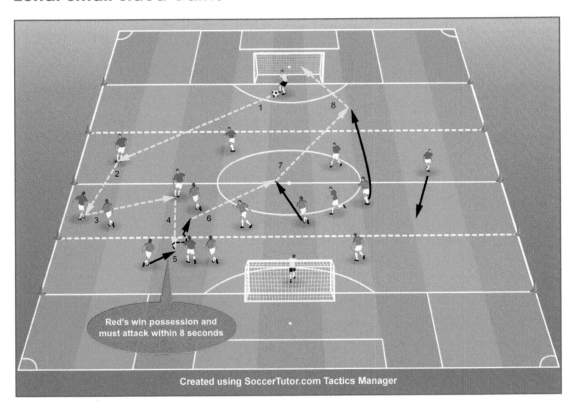

Red's win possession and must attack within 8 seconds

Created using SoccerTutor.com Tactics Manager

Description

Using a full sized pitch, mark out the area between the 2 penalty areas and divide into 4 equal zones as shown. Each team has different aims. The blues attack with no restrictions, while the reds have to defend with all their players in their own half or within the 2 central zones. If the reds win the ball, they have to finish their counter attack within 8 seconds.

Change the roles of the teams for the second set.

Variations

Limit number of players involved in counter attack; restrict number of touches for counter-attack; attacking players that are ahead of the ball cannot defend, etc.

Volume: 2 sets of 13 minutes with 2 minutes recovery time after each set.

FINAL PART OF THE SESSION: Stretching Exercises

BIBLIOGRAPHY

Abrantes, C.I., Nunes, M.I., Maças, V.M., Leite, N.M., Sampaio, J.E. (2012). Effects of the number of players and game type constraints on heart rate, rate of perceived exertion, and technical actions of small-sided soccer games. Journal of Strength and Conditioning Research, 26, 976-981.

Accame, F. (1995). Fútbol en zona. Madrid (Spain): Gymnos.

Achten, J., Jeukendrup, A. (2003). Heart rate monitoring: Applications and limitations. Sports Medicine, 33, 517- 538.

Árnason, A., Andersen, T.E., Holme, I., Engebretsen, L., Bahr, R. (2008). Prevention of hamstring strains in elite soccer: an intervention study. Scandinavian Journal of Medicine and Science in Sports, 18, 40-48.

Astorino, T., Tam, P.A., Rietschel, J.C., Johnson, S.M., Freedman, T.P. (2004). Changes in physical fitness parameters during a competitive field hockey season. Journal of Strength and Conditioning Research, 18, 850-854.

Askling, C., Karlsson, J., Thorstensson, A. (2003). Hamstring injury occurrence in elite soccer after preseason strength training with eccentric overload. Scandinavian Journal of Medicine and Science in Sports, 13, 244-250.

Athletes Performance (2011). Phase I Performance Mentorship. London (United Kingdom): Athletes Performance.

Baker, D. (2001). The effects of an in-season of concurrent training on the maintenance of maximal strength and power in professional and college-aged rugby league football players. Journal of Strength and Conditioning Research, 15, 172-177.

Baker, D., Wilson, G., Caylon, R. (1994). Periodization: the effect on strength of manipulating volume and intensity. Journal of Strength and Conditioning Research, 8, 235-242.

Balsom, P.D., Seger, J.Y., Sjödin, B., Ekblom, B. (1992a). Physiological responses to maximal intensity intermittent exercise. European Journal of Applied Physiology, 65, 144-149.

Balsom, P.D., Seger, J.Y., Sjödin, B., Ekblom, B. (1992b). Maximal-intensity intermittent exercise: Effect of recovery duration. International Journal of Sports Medicine, 13, 528-533.

Bangsbo, J. (1994a). Fitness training in football: A scientific approach. Bagsvaerd (Denmark): HO+ Storm.

Bangsbo, J. (1994b). Physiological demands. In Football (soccer) (edited by B. Ekblom), pp. 43-58. Oxford (United Kingdom): Blackwell.

Bangsbo, J. (1994c). The physiology of soccer – with special reference to intense intermittent exercise. Acta Physiologica Scandinavica, 151 (supp. 619).

Bangsbo, J. (2003). Integration of science in the training of elite football players. In Book of abstracts of the Vth World Congress on Science & Football, pp. 13. Madrid (Spain): Gymnos.

Bangsbo, J. (2004). Fatigue during a soccer match. Abstract from the communication presented to the International Congress The Rehabilitation of Sports Muscle and Tendon Injuries.

Bangsbo, J., Madsen, K., Kiens, B, Richer, E.A. (1996). Effect of muscle acidity on muscle metabolism and fatigue during intense exercise in man. Journal of Physiology, 495, 587-596.

Bartlett, R. (2001). Performance analysis: can bringing together biomechanics and notational analysis benefit coaches? International Journal of Performance Analysis in Sport, 1, 122-126.

Batty, E. (1980). Soccer coaching: The European way. London (United Kingdom): Souvenir Press.

Bondarchuk, A.P. (1988). Constructing a training system. Track Technique, 102, 254-269.

Bompa, T. (1999). Theory and methodology of training (4th Edition). Champaign (Illinois, United States): Human Kinetics.

Bradley, P.S., Sheldon, W., Wooster, B., Olsen, P., Boanas, P., Krustrup, P. (2009). High-intensity running in English FA Premier League soccer matches. Journal of Sports Sciences, 27, 159-168.

Campos, C. (2007). A singularidade da intervecao do treinador como a sua "impresao digital". Justificacao da periodizacao táctica como una "fenomenotecnica". Academic thesis. University of Porto (Portugal).

Cano, O. (2009). El modelo de juego del F.C. Barcelona. Vigo (Spain): MC Sports.

Caraffa, A., Cerulli, G., Projetti, M., Aisa, G., Rizzo, A. (1996). Prevention of anterior cruciate ligament injuries in soccer. A prospective controlled study of propioceptive training. Knee Surgery, Sports Traumatology & Arthroscopy, 4, 19-21.

Carli, G., Di Prisco, C.L., Martelli, G., Viti, A. (1982). Hormonal changes in soccer players during an agonistic season. Journal of Sports Medicine and Physical Fitness, 22, 489-494.

Carling, C., Bloomfield, J., Nelsen, L., Reilly, T. (2008). The role of motion analysis in elite soccer: contemporary performance measurement techniques and work rate data. Sports Medicine, 38, 839-862.

Casamichana, D., Castellano, J., Calleja, J., Román, J.S., Castagna, C. (2012). Relationship between indicators of training load in soccer players. Journal of Strength and Conditioning Research. In press.

Colli, R., Marra, E., Savoia, C., Azzone, V. (2011). La rivoluzione della misurazione della potenza metabolica nel calcio tramite gps o videoananalisi. In http://www.robertosassi.it.

Csikszentmihalyi, M. (1990). Flow: The psychology of optimal experience. New York (New York, United States): Harper and Row.

Dadebo, B., White, J., George, K.P. (2004). A survey of flexibility training protocols and hamstring strains in professional football clubs in England. British Journal of Sports Medicine, 38, 388-394.

Damasio, A.R. (2005). En busca de Spinoza: Neurobiología de la emoción y de los sentimientos. Barcelona (Spain): Crítica.

Da Silva, J.F., Guglielmo, L.G, Bishop, D. (2010). Relationship between different measures of aerobic fitness and repeated-sprint ability in elite soccer players. Journal of Strength and Conditioning Research, 24, 2115-2121.

Dawson, B., Fitzsimons, M., Ward, D. (1993). The relationship of repeated sprint ability to aerobic power and performance measures of anaerobic work capacity and power. Australian Journal of Science and Medicine in Sport, 25, 88-93.

Dellal, A., Chamari, K., Wong, D.P., Ahmaidi, S., Keller, D., Barros, R., Bisciotti, G.N., Carling, C. (2011a). Comparison of physical and technical performance in European soccer match-play: FA Premier League and La Liga. European Journal of Sports Sciences, 11, 51-59.

Dellal. A., Lago-Peñas, C., Wong, D.P., Chamari, K. (2011b). Effect of the number of ball contacts within bouts of 4 vs. 4 small-sided soccer games. International Journal of Sports Physiology and Performance, 6, 322-333.

Dellal, A., Chamari, K., Owen, A.L., Wong, D.P., Lago-Peñas, C., Hill-Haas, S. (2011c). Influence of the technical instructions on the physiological and physical demands within small sided soccer games. European Journal of Sports Sciences, 11, 353-358.

Dellal, A., Drust, B., Lago-Peñas, C. (2012a). Variation of activity demands in small-sided soccer games. International Journal of Sports Medicine, 33, 370-375.

Dellal, A., Owen, A., Wong, D.P., Krustrup, P., Van Exsel, M., Mallo, J. (2012b). Technical and physical demands of small vs. large sided games in relation to player position in elite soccer. Human Movement Science. In Press.

Díaz Otáñez, J. (1982). Manual de entrenamiento. Córdoba (Argentina): Jado.

Díaz Galán, I. (2012). Entrevista a Vitor Frade. In http://afluentesdelfutbol.blogspot.com.es/2012/03/vitor-fradeelpadre- de-la-periodizacion.html.

Di Salvo, V., Gregson, W., Atkinson, G., Tordoff, P., Drust, B. (2009). Analysis of high intensity activity in Premier League soccer. International Journal of Sports Medicine, 30, 205-212.

Dupont, G., Akakpo, K., Berthoin, S. (2004). The effect of in-season, high-intensity interval training in soccer players. Journal of Strength and Conditioning Research, 18, 584-589.

Dupont, G., Nedelec, M., McCall, A., McCormack, D., Berthoin, S., Wisloff, U. (2010). Effect of 2 soccer matches in a week on physical performance and injury rate. American Journal of Sports Medicine, 38, 1752-1758.

Dvorak, J., Junge, A., Derman, W., Schwellnuss, M. (2011). Injuries and illnesses of football players during the 2010 FIFA World Cup. British Journal of Sports Medicine, 45, 626-630.

Eirale, C., Hamilton, B., Bisciotti, G., Grantham, J., Chalabi H. (2012). Injury epidemiology in a national football team of the Middle East. Scandinavian Journal of Medicine and Science in Sports, 22, 323-329.

Ekstrand, J. (2008). Epidemiology of football injuries. Science & Sports, 23(2), 73-77.

Ekstrand, J., Timpka, T., Hägglund M. (2006). Risk of injury in elite football played on artificial turf versus natural grass: a prospective two-cohort study. British Journal of Sports Medicine, 40, 975-980.

Ekstrand, J., Hägglund, M., Waldén M. (2011). Epidemiology of muscle injuries in professional football (soccer). American Journal of Sports Medicine, 39, 1226-1232.

Espar, X. (2010). Jugar con el corazón. Barcelona (Spain): Plataforma Editorial.

Fitzsimons, M., Dawson, B., Ward, D., Wilkinson, A. (1993). Cycling and running test of repeated sprint ability. Australian Journal of Science and Medicine in Sport, 43, 14-20.

Fuller, C.W., Smith, G.L., Junge, A., Dvorak, J. (2004). The influence of tackle parameters on the propensity for injury in international football. American Journal of Sports Medicine, 32 (Suppl. 43), 43-53.

Fuller, C.W., Ekstrand, J., Junge, A., Andersen, T.E., Bahr, R., Dvorak, J, Hägglund, M., McCrory, P., Meeuwisse, W.H. (2006). Consensus statement on injury definitions and data collection procedures in studies of football (soccer) injuries. British Journal of Sports Medicine, 40, 193-201.

Gamble, P. (2006). Periodization training for team sport athletes. Strength and Conditioning Journal, 28 (5), 56-66.

Garganta, J., Oliveira, J. (1997). Estratégia e táctica nos jogos desportivos colectivos. Oporto (Portugal): University of Porto.

Gorostiaga, E.M., Izquierdo, M., Ruesta, M., Iribarren, J., González Badillo, J.J., Ibáñez, J. (2004). Strength training effects on physical performance and serum hormones in young soccer players. European Journal of Applied Physiology, 91, 698-707.

Gorostiaga, E.M., Granados, C., Ibáñez, J., González-Badillo, J.J., Izquierdo, M. (2006). Effects of an entire season on physical fitness changes in elite male handball players. Medicine and Science in Sports and Exercise, 38, 357-366.

Hägglund, M., Waldén, M., Bahr, R., Ekstrand, J. (2005). Methods for epidemiological study of injuries to professional football players: Developing the UEFA model. British Journal of Sports Medicine, 39, 340-346.

Hägglund, M., Waldén, M., Ekstrand J. (2006). Previous injury as a risk factor for injury in elite football: a prospective study over two consecutive seasons. British Journal of Sports Medicine, 40, 767-772.

Hägglund, M., Waldén, M., Ekstrand J. (2009). Injuries among male and female elite football players. Scandinavian Journal of Medicine and Science in Sports, 19, 751-752.

Hakkinen, K. (1993). Changes in physical fitness profile in female volleyball players during the competitive season. Journal of Sports Medicine and Physical Fitness, 33, 223-232.

Harre, D. (1982). Trainingslehre. Berlin (Germany): Sportverlag.

Helgerud, J., Engen, L.C., Wisloff, U., Hoff, J. (2001). Aerobic endurance training improves soccer performance. Medicine and Science in Sports and Exercise, 33, 1925-1931.

Hill-Haas, S., Coutts, A.J., Dawson, B.T., Rowsell, G.K. (2010). Time motion characteristics and physiological responses of small-sided games in elite youth players; the influence of player number and rule changes. Journal of Strength and Conditioning Research, 24, 2149-2156.

Hill-Haas, S., Dawson, B., Impellizzeri, F.M., Coutts, A. (2011). Physiology of small –sided games training in football: a systematic review. Sports Medicine, 41, 199-220.

Hoff, J., Wisloff, U., Engen, L.C., Kemi, O.J., Helgerud, J. (2002). Soccer specific aerobic endurance training. British Journal of Sports Medicine, 36, 218-221.

Hölmich, P., Uhrskou, P., Ulnits, L., Kanstrup, I.L., Nielsen, M.B., Bjerg, A.M., Krogsgaard, K. (1999). Effectiveness of active physical training as treatment for long-standing adductor-related groin pain in athletes: randomised trial. Lancet, 353, 439-443.

Impellizzeri, F.M., Rampinini, E., Coutts, A.J., Sassi, A., Marcora, S.M. (2004). Use of RPE-based training load in soccer. Medicine and Science in Sports and Exercise, 36, 1042-1047.

Impellizzeri, F.M., Marcora, S.M., Castagna, C., Reilly, T., Sassi, A., Iaia, F.M. (2006). Physiological and performance effects of generic versus specific aerobic training in soccer players. International Journal of Sports Medicine, 27, 483- 492.

Issurin, V. (2008). Block periodization versus traditional training theory: a review. Journal of Sports Medicine and Physical Fitness, 48, 65-75.

Issurin, V. (2010). New horizons for the methodology and physiology of training periodization. Sports Medicine, 40, 189-206.

Issurin, V., Kaverin, V. (1985). Planning and design of annual preparation cycle in caneo-kayak paddling. Moscow (Russia): Grebnoj Sport.

Junge, A., Rosch, D., Peterson, L., Graf-Baumann, T., Dvorak, J. (2002). Prevention of soccer injuries: a prospective intervention study in youth amateur players. American Journal of Sports Medicine, 30, 652-659.

Kelly, D.M., Drust, B. (2009). The effect of pitch dimensions on heart rate responses and technical demands of small-sided soccer games in elite players. Journal of Science and Medicine in Sport, 12, 475-479.

162

Knicker, A.J., Renshaw, I., Oldham, A.R., Cairns, S.P. (2011). Interactive processes link the multiple symptoms of fatigue in sport competition. Sports Medicine, 41, 307-328.

Kraemer, W.J., French, D.N., Paxton, N.J., Häkkinen, K., Volek, J.S., Sebastianelli, W.J. (2004). Changes in exercise performance and hormonal concentrations over a big ten soccer season in starters and nonstarters. Journal of Strength and Conditioning Research, 18, 121-128.

Krustrup, P., Mohr, M., Amstrup, T., Rysgaard, T., Johansen, J., Steensberg, A., Pedersen, P.K., Bangsbo, J. (2003). The Yo-yo intermittent recovery test: physiological response, reliability, and validity. Medicine and Science in Sports and Exercise, 35, 697-705.

Krustrup, P., Mohr, M., Steensberg, A., Bencke, J, Kjaer, M., Bangsbo, J. (2004). Muscle metabolites during a football match in relation to a decreased sprint ability. Journal of Sport Sciences, 22, 549.

Lago, C. (2009). The influence of match location, quality of opposition, and match status on possession strategies in professional association football. Journal of Sports Sciences, 27, 1463-1469.

Lago, C., Martín, R. (2007). Determinants of possession of the ball in soccer. Journal of Sports Sciences, 25, 969-974.

Little, T., Williams, A.G. (2007). Measures of exercise intensity during soccer training drills with professional soccer players. Journal of Strength and Conditioning Research, 21, 367-371.

Mahlo, F. (1969). La acción táctica en juego. La Habana (Cuba): Pueblo y Educación.

Mallo, J. (2006). Análisis del rendimiento físico de los árbitros y árbitros asistentes durante la competición en el fútbol. Doctoral Thesis. Universidad Politécnica de Madrid (Spain).

Mallo, J. (2011). Effect of block periodization on performance in competition in a soccer team during four consecutive seasons: A case study. International Journal of Performance Analysis in Sport, 11, 476-485.

Mallo, J. (2012a). Incidencia lesional en los futbolistas: Segunda División "B". Revista de Preparación Física en el Fútbol, 3, 84-95.

Mallo, J. (2012b). Effect of block periodization on physical fitness during a competitive soccer season. International Journal of Performance Analysis in Sport, 12, 64-74.

Mallo, J., Navarro, E. (2008). Physical load imposed on soccer players during small-sided training games. Journal of Sports Medicine and Physical Fitness, 48, 166-171.

Mallo, J., Navarro, E., García-Aranda, J. M., Gilis, B., Helsen, W. (2007). Activity profile of top-class soccer referees in relation to performance in selected physical tests. Journal of Sports Sciences, 25, 805-813.

Mallo, J., Navarro, E., García-Aranda, J.M., Helsen, W. (2009). Activity profile of top-class association football referees in relation to fitness-test performance and match standard. Journal of Sports Sciences, 27, 9-17.

Mallo, J., Gonzalez, P., Veiga, S., Navarro, E. (2011). Injury incidence in a Spanish sub-elite professional team: a prospective study during four competitive seasons. Journal of Sport Sciences and Medicine, 10, 731-736.

Mallo, J., Dellal, A. (2012). Injury risk in professional football players with special reference to the playing position and training periodization. Journal of Sports Medicine and Physical Fitness. In press.

Marcora, S.M., Staiano, W., Manning, V. (2009). Mental fatigue impairs physical performance in humans. Journal of Applied Physiology, 2009, 106, 857-864.

Matsui, T., Soya, S., Okamoto, M., Ichitani, Y., Kawanaka, K., Soya, H. (2011). Brain glycogen decreases during prolonged exercise. Journal of Physiology, 589, 3383-3393.

Matsui, T., Ishikawa, T., Ito, H., Okamoto, M., Inoue, K., Lee, M., Fujikawa, T., Ichitani, Y., Kawakana, K., Soya, H. (2012). Brain glycogen supercompensation following exhaustive exercise. Journal of Physiology, 590, 607-616.

Matveiev, L.P. (1981). Fundamentals of sport training. Moscow (Russia): Progress Publishers.

Meckel, Y., Machnai, O., Eliakim, A. (2009). Relationship among repeated sprint tests aerobic fitness, and anaerobic fitness in elite adolescent soccer players. Journal of Strength and Conditioning Research, 23, 163-169.

Mjolsnes, R., Arnason, A., Osthagen, T., Raastad, T., Bahr R. (2004). A 10-week randomized trial comparing eccentric vs concentric hamstring strength training in well-trained soccer players. Scandinavian Journal of Medicine and Science in Sports, 14, 311-317.

Miñano, J. (2006). Medidas adaptativas en la planificación del entrenamiento en equipos con alta densidad competitiva. Master in Fitness training in football. Real Federación Española de Fútbol – Universidad de Castilla La Mancha (Spain).

Mohr, M., Krustrup, P., Bangsbo, J. (2003). Match performance of high-standard soccer players with special reference to development of fatigue. Journal of Sports Sciences, 21, 519-528.

Mohr, M., Krustrup, P., Bangsbo, J. (2005). Fatigue in soccer: A brief review. Journal of Sports Sciences, 23, 593-599.

Morgan, B.E., Oberlander, M.A. (2001). An examination of injuries in Major League Soccer. The Inaugural season. American Journal of Sports Medicine, 29, 426-430.

Mújika, I. (2009). Tapering and peaking for optimal performance. Leeds (United Kingdom): Human Kinetics.

Mújika, I., Padilla S (2003). Scientific bases for precompetition tapering strategies. Medicine and Science in Sports and Exercise, 35, 1182-1187.

Navarro, F. (2001). Principios del entrenamiento y estructuras de la planificación deportiva. Master in High performance in sports. Comité Olímpico Español – Universidad Autónoma de Madrid (Spain).

Newton, R.U., Rogers, R.A., Volek, J.S. (2006). Four weeks of optimal resistance training at the end of the season attenuates declining of jump performance of women volleyball players. Journal of Strength and Conditioning Research, 20, 955-961.

Nordsborg, N., Mohr, M., Pedersen, L.D., Nielsen, J.J., Bangsbo, J. (2003). Muscle interstitial potassium kinetics during intense exhaustive exercise – effect of previous arm exercise. American Journal of Physiology, 285, 143-148.

North, J.S., Williams, A.M., Hodges, N., Ward, P., Ericsson, K.A. (2009). Perceiving patterns in dynamic action sequences: The relationship between anticipation and pattern recognition skill. Applied Cognitive Psychology, 23, 878-894.

Noya, J., Sillero, M. (2012). Incidencia lesional en el fútbol profesional español a lo largo de una temporada: días de baja por lesión. Apunts Medicina Esport. In press.

Oliveira, B., Amieiro, N., Resende, N., Barreto, R. (2007). Mourinho ¿Por qué tantas victorias? Vigo (Spain): MC Sports.

Osgnach, C., Poser, S., Bernardini, R., Rinaldo, R., di Prampero, P.E. (2010). Energy cost and metabolic power in elite soccer: a new match analysis approach. Medicine and Science in Sports and Exercise, 42, 170-178.

Owen, A.L., Twist, C., Ford, P. (2004). Small-sided games: the physiological and technical effect of altering pitch size and player numbers. Insight: The F.A. Coaches Association Journal, 7, 50-53.

Periodization Fitness Training

Owen, A.L., Wong, P., McKenna, M., Dellal, A. (2011). Heart rate responses and technical comparison between small- vs. large-sided games in elite professional soccer. Journal of Strength and Conditioning Research, 25, 2104- 2110.

Paredes, V. (2009). Método de cuantificación en la readaptación de lesiones en fútbol. Doctoral Thesis. Universidad Autónoma de Madrid (Spain).

Platonov, V.N. (1988). El entrenamiento deportivo: Teoría y Metodología. Barcelona (Spain): Paidotribo.

Pol, R. (2011). La Preparación ¿Física? en el fútbol. Vigo (Spain): MC Sports.

Punset, E. (2010). Viaje a las emociones. Barcelona (Spain): Destino.

Punset, E. (2011). Excusas para no pensar. Barcelona (Spain): Destino.

Rahnama, N., Reilly, T., Lees, A., Graham-Smith, P. (2003). Muscle fatigue induced by exercise simulating the work rate of competitive soccer. Journal of Sports Sciences, 21, 933-942.

Rampinini, E., Sassi, A., Sassi, R., Impellizzeri, F.M. (2004). Variables influencing fatigue in soccer performance. Abstract from the communication presented to the International Congress The Rehabilitation of Sports Muscle and Tendon Injuries.

Reep, C., Benjamin, B. (1968). Skill and chance in Association Football. Journal of the Royal Statistical Society Series, 131, 581-585.

Roca, A. (2011). El proceso de entrenamiento en el fútbol. Vigo (Spain): MC Sports.

Ruíz Pérez, L.M. (1994). Deporte y aprendizaje. Madrid (Spain): Visor.

Sánchez Bañuelos, F. (1997). Didáctica de la Educación Física y el Deporte. INEF Madrid (Spain).

Sanz, J.M. (2010). Una manera de entender el entrenamiento en el fútbol. Presentation in the Master in Fitness training in football. Real Federación Española de Fútbol – Universidad de Castilla La Mancha (Spain).

Sampedro, J. (1999). Fundamentos de táctica deportiva. Análisis de la estrategia en los deportes. Madrid (Spain): Gymnos.

San Román, Z. (2003) Causas de las bajas a entrenamientos y competiciones profesionales de los futbolistas profesionales con unas cargas determinadas de trabajo. Doctoral Thesis. Universidad de Extremadura (Spain).

Schneider, V., Arnold, B., Martin, K., Bell, D., Crocker, P. (1998). Detraining effect in college football players during the competitive season. Strength and Conditioning Journal, 12, 42-45.

Seirul·lo, F. (1987). Opción de planificación en los deportes de largo período de competiciones. Revista de Entrenamiento Deportivo, I (3), 53-62.

Seirul·lo, F. (1994). Criterios modernos de entrenamiento en el fútbol. In Jornadas internacionales de medicina y fútbol premundial 94 (pp. 201-212). Vitoria (Spain): Instituto Vasco de Educación Física.

Seirul·lo, F. (2001). Entrevista de metodología y planificación. Training Futbol, 65, 8-17.

Seirul·lo, F. (2003). Planificación del Entrenamiento. Professional Master in High performance in team sports. Barcelona (Spain): CEDE.

Selye, H. (1950). Stress and general adaptation syndrome. British Journal of Medicine, 1 (4667), 1383-1392.

Solé, J. (2002). Fundamentos del entrenamiento deportivo. Barcelona (Spain): Ergo.

Solé, J. (2003). Entrenamiento de la resistencia en los deportes de equipo. Professional Master in High performance in team sports. Barcelona (Spain): CEDE.

Solé, J. (2006). Planificación del entrenamiento deportivo. Barcelona (Spain): Sicropat Sport.

Solé, J. (2008). Teoría del entrenamiento deportivo. Barcelona (Spain): Sicropat Sport.

Stolen, T., Chamari, K., Castagna, C., Wisloff, U. (2005). Physiology of soccer: An update. Sports Medicine, 35, 501- 536.

Tamarit, X. (2007). ¿Qué es la periodización táctica? Vigo (Spain): MC Sports.

Tenga, A., Holme, I., Ronglan, L.T., Bahr, R. (2010. Effects of playing tactics on goal scoring in Norwegian professional soccer. Journal of Sports Sciences, 28, 237-244.

Touretski, G. (1998). Preparation of sprints events. 1998 ASCTA Convention. Camberra (Australia): Australian Institute of Sport.

Vaeyens, R., Lenoir, M., Williams, A.M., Mazyn, L., Philippaerts, R.M. (2007). The effects of task constraints on visual search behaviour and decision-making skill in youth soccer players. Journal of Sports and Exercise Psychology, 29: 147-169.

Verjoshanski, I.V. (1990). Entrenamiento deportivo, planificación y programación. Barcelona (Spain): Martínez Roca.

Waldén, M., Hägglund, M., Ekstrand J. (2005). UEFA Champions League study: a prospective study of injuries in professional football during the 2001-2002 season. British Journal of Sports Medicine, 39, 542-546.

Ward, P., Williams, A.M., Hancock, P. (2006). Simulation for performance and training. En: Ericsson K.A., Charness, N., Feltovich, P.J., Hoffman P. (Ed.), The Cambridge handbook of expertise and expert performance (pp. 243-262). Cambridge: Cambridge University Press.

Weineck, J. (1988). Entrenamiento óptimo. Barcelona (Spain): Hispano Europea.

Williams, A.M., Ford, P.F., Eccles, D.W., Ward, P. (2011). Perceptual-cognitive expertise in sport and its acquisition: Implications for applied cognitive psychology. Applied Cognitive Psychology, 25, 432-442.

Wisloff, U., Castagna, C., Helgerud, J., Jones, R., Hoff, J. (2004). Maximal squat strength is strongly correlated to sprint-performance and vertical jump height in elite soccer players. British Journal of Sports Medicine, 38: 285-288.

Witvrouw, E., Daneels, L., Asselman, P., D´Have, T., Cambier, D. (2003). Muscle flexibility as a risk factor for developing muscular injuries in male professional soccer players. American Journal of Sports Medicine, 31, 41-46.

Woods, C., Hawkins, R.D., Maltby, S., Hulse, M., Thomas, A., Hodson A. (2004). The Football Association Medical Research Programme: An audit to injuries in professional football – analysis of hamstring injuries. British Journal of Sports Medicine, 38, 36-41.

Zubillaga, A. (2006). La actividad del jugador de fútbol en alta competición: Análisis de variabilidad. Doctoral Thesis. Universidad de Málaga (Spain).

Zubillaga, A., Gorospe, G., Hernández-Mendo, A., Blanco-Villanesor, A. (2008). Comparative analysis of the highintensity activity of soccer players in top-level competition. In Science and football VI (edited by T. Reilly & F. Korkusuz), pp. 182-186. Abingdon (United Kingdom): Routledge.

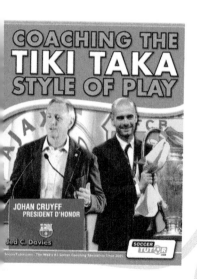

CPSIA information can be obtained
at www.ICGtesting.com
Printed in the USA
LVOW05s0017231115

R10257700001B/R102577PG463470LVX1B/1/P